Elk Mountains Odyssey

An Historical Perspective of the West Elk Loop
A Travel Guide for the West Elk Loop Scenic and Historic Byw

Over Mountains High they went
On the quest for treasure bent;
Climbing hills and fording streams,
Fighting hardships, dreaming dreams...
　　　　　　　　-Len Shoemaker

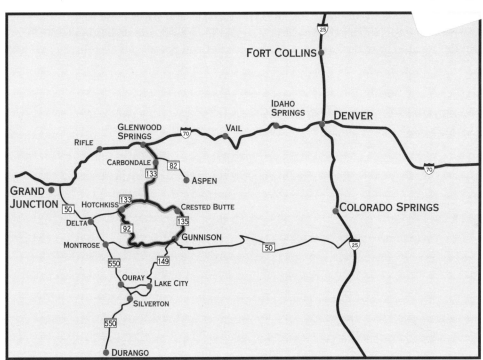

A Forest Service Ranger describes the West Elk Loop as "the closest you can come to a wilderness experience in a passenger car." Considering that the route circumnavigates one large designated Wilderness Area - the West Elk - and skirts four others, the Maroon Bells - Snowmass, The Raggeds, Black Canyon of the Gunnison and Fossil Ridge, plus thousands of acres of National Forest - the statement is without exaggeration.

The West Elk Loop, one of 21 scenic byways designated by the State of Colorado, covers 204 miles of two-lane road through rural western Colorado. Not all the route is paved, and little of it is flat or straight. The drama of the terrain is reflected in the contours of the byway as it carves along canyon rims, edges along coursing rivers, cuts through the dappled shade of evergreens and aspen, and cleaves through desert and sagebrush plains.

The route follows the narrow alignment of long gone railroad grades, the faint hoof prints of the earliest explorers, and the ancient pathways of Ute Indians. Less than 150 years ago, the country seen from the West Elk Loop was a great, unspoiled wilderness, and in many places still is.

ORIENTATION

Section I begins in Carbondale, where the Byway starts at the intersection of Colorado State Highways 82 and 133. It follows Highway 133 south up the Crystal River, over McClure Pass, through "the Muddy" region and down to Paonia Reservoir and Dam.

Section II heads west into the coal mining area of the North Fork Valley of the Gunnison River and to Paonia and Hotchkiss, fabled fruit producing areas.

The route then veers south from Hotchkiss on Highway 92 to climb through rolling ranch land to Crawford.

Section III passes Crawford Reservoir and crests on the rim of the Black Canyon of the Gunnison. There it carves a serpentine path across Black Mesa, always with spectacular views of the canyons and hundreds of square miles of mountain scenery, including the San Juan Mountains to the south. It joins U.S. Highway 50 at Blue Mesa

Dam and follows it east along Blue Mesa Reservoir to Gunnison.

Section IV ventures north on Highway 135 along the Gunnison River to Almont, then up the East River Valley to Crested Butte.

Section V visits Crested Butte and the nearby area, then turns west over Kebler Pass, a summer-only dirt road that easily accommodates the average passenger car. Crystal Meadows is the end of the loop at the Paonia Reservoir Dam.

Each section is organized for both ease of reading and for entry anywhere on the Byway; the color tabs on each right hand page let travelers quickly find the Byway section they happen to be driving. Listings of scenic and historic points of interest are at the back of each section of the Byway.

The locator map provides a graphic overview of the Byway. Each section has a strip map for that part of the route to help locate points of interest.

The West Elk Loop is a transportation connector between these diverse geographic zones. Each section exhibits distinguishing characteristics. One is geology.

Geology of the West Elk Loop

THE CRYSTAL VALLEY

Carbondale is built on an alluvial plain created by the Crystal and Roaring Fork rivers, which deposited sediments on the evaporites of a Paleozoic sea bottom surrounded by red desert sediments that originally gave Colorado its Spanish name, "reddish color". On its 40-mile

DENVER PUBLIC LIBRARY

Prospectors were among the earliest arrivals in the Elk Mountains, accompanied by faithful burros which packed the supplies and necessities each person needed. They were part of the transportation system of the day.

course from the high basins of the Elk Mountains near Schofield Pass to its joining with the Roaring Fork River at Carbondale, the Crystal River carries snowmelt and carves through complex structures and unwarped sediments of the Colorado Plateau, known as the Grand Hogback. The river is the dividing line between the brightly colored sediments of the Grand Hogback, on the fringe of the extensive Colorado Plateau to the west, and the crystalline Elk Mountains to the east which the Hayden Survey of 1870 labeled one of the most highly mineralized and complex geological areas in the U.S.

Mt. Sopris (12,953 ft.) rises dramatically above Carbondale. This lacolith, an igneous intrusive, was pushed up in the Cenozoic era 70 million years ago through shale, then weathered into the formidable mountain peak that dominates the lower Crystal valley. South of Mt. Sopris, the Crystal cascades through a granite gate at Penny Hot Springs and again through the Maroon Formation near Redstone. Penny Hot Springs surfaces in a steam cloud along the Crystal with 120-plus degree water. The spring is located on the contact between the Mt. Sopris intrusion and the sedimentary sandstone upthrust of the Maroon Formation.

Rising past Placita the valley flattens in a broad expanse of alluvial basins and glacial fill as far as the ramparts of Chair Mountain (12,721 ft.), an impressive igneous intrusive. Following the Crystal River east, the river churns through narrow gorges above Marble and collects rushing tributaries near Crystal City.

Chair Mountain, Highway 133 before it was paved, the Crystal River and an old county road paint a vivid picture of travel problems in earlier days.

Bicycling was a mode of travel even before today's exotic wheels.

Along its upper course, gold, lead, zinc and copper are found, and at Marble vast stores of metamorphosed limestone furnish the country's finest marble. Coal, metamorphosed into high quality coking bituminous, is imbedded in fields near Redstone and Placita, and at Thompson Creek, near Carbondale.

The rich mineral deposits of the upper Crystal spurred development at the headwaters first and fashioned a down-valley progression of settlements.

THE WEST ELKS

Climbing over McClure Pass, the route crosses an ancient shoreline of the coal-bearing Mesa Verde sandstones and dark gray Mancos shale, which continue through the Muddy Region and into the North Fork Valley.

From the Ruby Range at the northern end of the West Elk Mountains near Kebler Pass to the Black Canyon of the Gunnison on the south, major upheavals created a rugged landscape that would challenge the ingenuity and strength of pioneers while gracing this portion of Colorado's Western Slope with awe-inspiring beauty.

The West Elks are described as a "30-mile-long bulge of molten rock" that tried to push up beneath thousands of feet of shale. At the present location of West Elk Peak (13,035 ft.), northwest of Gunnison,

Skiing in the rugged, snow clad Elk Mountains was transportation in the 1880's. Now it is recreation.

The Hayden Survey explored, mapped and reported on the minerals of the Elk Mountains. Hayden and his Rover Boys were among the earliest visitors to the region. William Henry Jackson photo.

the molten rock reached the surface 30 million years ago in a massive volcano that melted ice and snow and caused major mudslides. This mud weathered into spires and cliffs, like the Palisades west of Gunnison and the Dillon Pinnacles at Blue Mesa.

Another feature of volcanism and weathering is seen in the many dikes and sills of volcanic rock that were pushed up as molten magma, then weathered out of the softer, surrounding rock. The Dike, near Horse Ranch Park on Kebler Pass, is a long magma upthrust that crosses the valley like a broken down wall and climbs toward the ridge of 12,644-foot Ruby Peak. Needle Rock, east of Crawford, is a volcanic neck that stands as a dramatic butte.

The many mesas of the southern West Elks, nearer the Black Canyon, are remnants of mud flows from the West Elk volcano. These flat mesas were later capped by "welded tuff," the residue of "glowing avalanches" of volcanic ash from the San Juan Mountains to the south that hardened into an extremely durable rock. Weathering eroded softer rock and mud from the sides of the mesas, leaving more durable table tops separated by sheer walls and canyons.

In the northern West Elks, laccoliths, or bulges of magma, intruded into Mancos shale, creating huge humps of granite beneath 5,000 feet of shale overburden. The peaks around Kebler Pass and in the nearby Ohio Creek drainage are the domes of lacoliths exposed by erosion of shale, as are Round Mountain, Crested Butte Mountain, Snodgrass Hill and Gothic Mountain, which mark the eastern edge of the Elk Mountains at Crested Butte in the East River Valley.

GLACIATION

While upheavals and water erosion account for much of the topography along the route, glaciation gave it the finishing touches. The most recent ice age was the Wisconsin Ice Age which ended 10,000 years ago. Glaciers carved many of the U-shaped valleys above 9,000 feet, sculpted the "horns", or jagged mountain peaks, shaped the "aretes", or sharp ridges and excavated high alpine lakes. In their wake they left "moraines," the boulder-strewn rubble piles created by intensive grinding.

ELK MOUNTAINS ODYSSEY

THE WEST ELK LOOP
SCENIC AND HISTORIC BYWAY GUIDE

Paul Andersen and Ken Johnson

ABOUT THIS GUIDE

This guide book conveys more than the enormity and striking beauty of the landscape. Its purpose is to explore the history of a region that became the stage for a dramatic human experience described first by a painful clash of cultures–the expulsion of the Ute Indians and the ascendance of the white Europeans–followed by the struggle to tame a wild land and exploit its riches. Through these trials a land ethic has been established and a conservation effort born. The creation of Colorado's scenic and historic byways and the establishment of the West Elk Loop is a statement of lasting appreciation for what nature has endowed.

CREDITS

The West Elk Loop Scenic and Historic Byway is divided into three main regions: the Crystal Valley, the North Fork Valley and the Gunnison country. Getting designation of the Byway, followed by the vision for this book, has been guided by a Steering Committee representing each of the three planning and interpretive zones. This includes representatives from the Colorado Department of Transportation, U.S. Forest Service, National Park Service, Bureau of Land Management, Colorado Division of Wildlife, the University of Colorado and the Western Colorado Interpretive Association.

A federal grant plus help and funds from the Colorado Historical Society to the byway committee brought this book to reality.

Special thanks goes to the committee: Dorothea Farris, Kay Tennison, Susan Hansen, Tom Kuekes, Ray Kingston, Jo Feinauer, Dave Roberts, Jon Schler, Tammy Scott, Ray David, Larry Kontour, Diane Markowitz, Chris Chacos, Ron and Michelle Sorter, John and Pat Zollinger, Abbott Fay and John McEvoy, whose photography also graces these pages.

Their work and dedication to the West Elk Loop Scenic and Historic Byway is a lasting memorial and a major benefit to all who live and work along the byway and cherish its history.

This book would have been impossible without the many historians, researchers and scientists whose work is represented here. The authors' gratitude goes to Laura Clock, Len Shoemaker, Duane Vandenbusche, Thomas Prather, Muriel Marshall, George Sibley and Mamie Ferrier, Grant Ferrier, Don and Jean Grisswold, Claudia King, Berton Braley, Phyllis Flanders Dorset, John T. McMullan, George Crofutt, Sidney Jocknick, Betty Wallace, Ted Warner, Wallace Hansen, Mark Pearson, Jan Pettit, Carl Ubbelohde, Maxine Benson, Duane Smith, D. Ray Wilson, Mary Boland, Judy Livingston, Donna Daniels, Elaine Henderson, Steven Mehls, Russ Collman, James Johnson, Sylvia Ruland, Abbott Fay, John McEvoy, Carol Craven and historical societies and museums of Carbondale, Glenwood Springs, Aspen, Redstone, Hotchkiss, Paonia, Gunnison and Crested Butte.

Contributing special color and historical accuracy were Duane Vandenbusche, Abbott Fay, Grant and Mamie Ferrier and Laura Clock. Contribution of photographs from all sources has helped bring the past to life and preserve history.

About the authors: Paul Andersen is a veteran reporter and writer, now independently writing book projects, screenplays, magazine articles and a weekly column for the Aspen Times where he is a contributing editor. He is a graduate of Western State College, was a reporter for the Gunnison Country Times, editor of the Crested Butte Chronicle and was a reporter and editor for the Aspen Times. He rode his bicycle around the 204 miles of the West Elk Loop to capture the flavor of the country and its peoples.

Ken Johnson is a newspaperman who has owned and edited 17 newspapers from California to Florida, from Grand Junction, Colorado to Cleveland, Ohio. He has developed magazines, been a graphic arts consultant and has researched the history of the Crystal River Valley and Redstone for over 20 years. He also guides Redstone Press, book publishers.

Copyright © 1998 / All Rights Reserved
Redstone Press
Box 580
Carbondale, CO 81623

Cover Photograph: John McEvoy, a derelict cabin under the Raggeds tells of hopes and dreams
Back Cover Photographs: John McEvoy, Tom Kuekes
Book Design: Frank Gayer Martin

ISBN 0-9664445-0-7
LCCCCN 98-091476

President Theodore Roosevelt hunted on the north end of the West Elk Loop, and after this 1905 trip the "Teddy" bear came into being.

FLORA AND FAUNA

Aspect, elevation and climate determine the great variety of living creatures along the West Elk Loop, from pinon, juniper, cactus and sage brush in lower, south-facing desert regions to grassy tundra and wildflowers in the high alpine regions above timberline. Forests range from about 5,000 feet in the lower montane region where they mix with grasslands, shrublands and woodlands, and extend to roughly 11,500 feet. Between these extremes are found cottonwood, scrub oak, aspen, lodgepole pine, and "black timber" spruce forests.

The aspen tree is an unique organism that produces clones from common root systems and reproduces rapidly to cover vast areas. The largest contiguous aspen forest in the world, made up of many thousands of clone colonies, is found on the west side of Kebler Pass. Massive wildfires in the 1700s wiped out the black timber conifers and allowed the aspen to grow into major stands whose leaves "quake" during summer, turn bright yellow, orange and red in autumn, and stand denuded like so many porcupine quills in the winter.

Varied topography along the West Elk Loop creates numerous microclimates. Paonia is a "banana belt" where mild temperatures allow fruit growing, while Gunnison is a cold sink that creates a frigid icebox during winter months with temperatures down to 50 below. Carbondale has relatively scant snowfall, while nearby Redstone and Marble are often inundated. Crested Butte and Kebler Pass receive up to 350 inches of snow a year, while the adjacent North Fork Valley is mild and relatively dry.

Plant life along the route is incredibly abundant and diverse, with thousands of species of shrubs and wildflowers. The foothills and mountain valleys are colored by Blue Flax, Scarlet Gilia, Rabbit Brush and Shooting Stars. Higher, in the subalpine zone, the Pasque Flower and Skunk Cabbage appear through spring snow as the weather warms. They are joined by Mountain Lady's Slipper, Monkshood, Lupine, Aster, Elephanthead, Columbine, Fireweed and Arnica. On the highest slopes are Alpine Forget-Me-Nots, Sky Pilots, Avalanche Lilies, King's Crown and Arctic Gentian.

The Colorado Blue Columbine was discovered by botanist Edwin James in 1820 and protected by law in 1825. Illegal to pick in the wilds, it was decreed the State Flower of Colorado in 1899 and derives its name from the Latin word *colomba*, which means dove. Its long spurs and petals were thought to resemble a circle of doves dancing around the stem. The Utes used Columbine seeds for a tea that cured headaches and fevers.

Bird life is abundant in the beaver country along the river valleys, with ducks, blue herons, Canada geese, bald and golden eagles, water ouzels, a variety of hawks and owls, Canada jays, Stellar jays, magpies, hummingbirds, bluebirds, ravens, robins and many more. High-soaring birds like hawks and eagles are often seen playing among the mountain peaks on rising thermals.

Wildlife includes elk, mule deer, black bear, bighorn sheep, mountain goat, mountain lion, bobcat, ermine, beaver, muskrat, red fox, coyote, pine marten, raccoon, skunk and badger. Elk in the White River National Forest alone total an estimated 20,000 and comprise one of the largest herds in North America. Lakes and streams are home to rainbow trout, cutthroat trout, brook trout, lake trout, kokanee salmon and mountain whitefish.

THE WHITE RIVER AND GUNNISON NATIONAL FORESTS

Much of the open space and mountain scenery along the West Elk Loop is part of the 180 million-acre National Forest System administered by the Forest Service. Predicated on the "multiple use" concept, the mandate is that no single land use dominates the forest.

In the White River and Gunnison

Rocky Mountain Big Horn Sheep are commonly seen in the winter and spring.

Bears are among the many wild animals to be seen by the observant traveler.

National Forests early mining, fur trapping and timbering have given way to tourism and recreation, including hiking, backpacking, horseback riding, water sports, fishing, hunting, mountain biking, snowmobiling, four-wheeling, photography and skiing.

While trails and roads are numerous and well-suited to off-road vehicles, designated Wilderness areas have been established in both Forests to preserve and protect the pristine values of nature by banning motorized and mechanized vehicles. The West Elk Loop circles the West Elk Wilderness, and also skirts the Maroon Bells-Snowmass, the Raggeds, Black Canyon and Fossil Ridge Wilderness Areas. Each area affords a highly valued immersion into the natural world. Travel is limited to foot or horseback.

The two million acre White River National Forest administers lands along the West Elk Loop north of McClure Pass and including the northern Elk Mountains. This is one of the largest and oldest of the National Forests, created as a Federal timber reserve on October 16, 1891 by proclamation of President Benjamin Harrison.

The Crystal Valley follows the edge of the Maroon Bells-Snowmass Wilderness from Mt. Sopris to the Marble turnoff, some 25 miles way. The forest boundary sign is at old Janeway about 13 miles from the start of the Byway. White River National Forest offices are in Glenwood Springs and Carbondale.

First explored by John C. Fremont in 1845, the White River National Forest was a mining mecca until the silver crash of 1893. Among the personages who visited the White River Forest during its colorful history were Presidents U.S. Grant and Theodore Roosevelt, gunfighter "Doc" Holiday, and mining magnate Horace Tabor with his wife Baby "Doe".

The Gunnison National Forest, which hosts the southern part of the Loop,

Cold, wet and sweating all at the same time; that was the labor of the sluice box. Shoveling gold-bearing sand and gravel into the wooden box was one way of getting gold. Nuggets meant you had struck it rich!

"Frequently he hasn't a dollar, but he manages to live by taking odd jobs at working assessments, then lays in a supply of grub and tobacco, and he's fixed for another year. They are happy fellows, whole-souled and generous to the last pinch of flour and bacon rind. I love those fellows, the prospectors."

CAMPING

Summer camping abounds on the West Elk Loop, with numerous National, State and locally managed public campgrounds offering amenities and ready access to high mountain environments, lakes, streams and historic sites.

Forest Service campgrounds include Avalanche (mile 58), Redstone (mile 53) and Bogan Flats campgrounds (mile 45). They offer camping along Highway 133, the Crystal River corridor, in the White River National Forest between Carbondale and Marble.

In the Gunnison National Forest, nearest the West Elk Loop are McClure Campground (mile 41) near the top of McClure Pass; Erikson Springs Campground (mile 23) at the west end of Kebler Pass; Lake Irwin and Lost Lake Campgrounds high on Kebler Pass; Gothic, Avery Peak, and Cement Creek Campgrounds near Crested Butte; and North Bank, Spring Creek, Taylor Park, Onemile and Rosy Lane Campgrounds near Almont (mile 10, Highway 135).

Paonia State Park at Paonia Reservoir (mile 28) is managed by the Colorado Division of Parks and Outdoor Recreation and the U.S. Bureau of Reclamation. The park has 15 primitive campsites with no

including the southern Elk Mountains and the Sawatch Range, manages 1.7 million acres of outstanding mountain scenery. Its offices are in Gunnison and Paonia. It administers the Crested Butte Ski Area and a growing array of recreational uses and industrial interests.

THE ULTIMATE OPTIMISTS

From a 1916 edition of the Marble *Booster* comes a description that serves as a commemoration to one of the West's most enduring, courageous, adventuresome and foolhardy individuals. Without this character, the history of the West would have been markedly different.

"If you never saw an optimist in your life, go into one of these mining camps and you will find him in all his radiancy in the prospector who has been pegging away at a number of claims for lo, these many years, and is just on the verge of striking it rich.

THE CURSE OF THE UTES

In the Treaty of 1863 the Utes ceded eastern portions of their mountain homeland to the white settlers and miners who anxiously swarmed the region for mineral wealth and homestead land. In that treaty the Utes were promised the Crystal River valley would be theirs "for as long as the rivers might run and the grasses might grow." Subsequently, as part of a national policy where Indians were deemed to be in the way of settlement, that pledge was broken and the Utes were forced out of their cherished valley. When they left, the Utes are said to have placed a curse on the valley, a jinx that would frustrate any and all efforts of Whites to exploit its riches and establish settlements.

In the August 25, 1917 edition of the Marble Booster, a bankrupt newspaper editor, mourning a severe economic downturn, suggested that the curse was proven by the failure of four once-thriving towns in the Crystal Valley - Crystal City, Marble, Placita and Redstone.

Six Utes and a white man make a harmonious picture masking the push to move the Indians out of the way.

"First there was Crystal, once a mining town of several hundred souls and a metropolis for several other smaller mining camps. Then came Redstone, where millions of dollars were spent to make the prettiest, most ideal coal camp in the world. There was Placita, at one time a prosperous coal camp of several hundred, and where scarcely a remnant is left. Then comes Marble: Twelve millions of dollars are invested here in quarries and the finishing plant of the Colorado-Yule Marble Company, besides thousands upon thousands in stores and homes. Now there are scarcely 50 men in Marble. It is pitiful to contemplate such hard luck."

While the Crystal Valley today enjoys a resurgent economy based on tourism, the tides of success and failure run in a regular ebb and flow. Perhaps the Utes will have the final word after all if their curse remains "for as long as the rivers might run and the grasses might grow."

---

drinking water, a boat ramp, picnic areas and bathroom facilities. Entry fee is $4. Camping is an additional $6.

Crawford Reservoir, one mile south of Crawford on Highway 92 (Mile 33), is also managed by the Colorado Division of Parks and Outdoor Recreation. It has two campgrounds: Clear Fork, with 21 sites, and Iron Creek, with 45 sites. Both have ADA accessible facilities, showers and flush toilets, but only Iron Creek has water and electric hookups at each campsite.

There are two boat ramps with loading docks, a ski beach, a swimming beach and hiking trails. Entry fee is $4. Camping is $7 more at Clear Fork and $10 at Iron Creek.

The Black Canyon of the Gunnison National Monument, North Rim, is 11 miles from the turnoff on Highway 92, one mile south of Crawford. Follow the road to the North Rim and camp near spectacular Chasm View, a 2,000 foot drop straight down to the depths of the gorge where the Gunnison River churns through an incredible narrows.

A visitor center is located on the South Rim, near Montrose, where information, facilities and exhibits are provided. It is 90 miles of scenic driving around to the South Rim. The North Rim offers a more primitive and remote experience where a scenic drive and numerous

turnouts offer stunning views. For the adventuresome traveler there is a rough and tumble route to the bottom of the canyon down "S.O.B. Gully," an appropriately named scramble. A free back country permit may be obtained at the North Rim Ranger Station.

The Curecanti National Recreation Area near Gunnison on Highway 50 at Blue Mesa Reservoir offers eight campgrounds, two marinas, picnicking, hiking, boating, swimming, fishing, visitor's centers and campfire programs. The National Park Service administers Curecanti and Black Canyon. Headquarters are at Elk Creek, midway along the reservoir.

The 17 member Ute Indian delegation to Washington included Captain Jack, fourth from the left, and Buckskin Charley, fourth from the right. They were ordered to Washington in 1880 following the Meeker massacre. This meeting led to banishing the Utes to reservations in southern Colorado and eastern Utah.

The Ute Indians

The only Indians indigenous to Colorado, the Utes can be traced to early Fremont man, who migrated from the Bering Strait 10,000 years ago and occupied west-central Colorado as part of a desert culture which later produced the Anasazi. The Fremonts may have been the predecessors of the Shoshonean tribes, one of which became the primary occupant of Colorado - the Utes. As hunter gatherers, the Utes established seven major sub groups - the Uintahs, Yampas, Parianucs, Uncompahgres, Weeminuches, Capotes and Mouaches. Armed with bows and arrows, they were able hunters and feared warriors. Later they acquired horses from stock the Spaniards brought to the new land, and with guns they were masters of a virtual nation.

The Utes practiced a universal religion in a natural sanctuary of mountains, rivers and forests whose bounty allowed them a comfortable life. They sent prayers to spirits representing floods, thunder and lightning, and wild game. They appealed to a spirit of the blood to ward off sickness, and based their spirituality on the natural world around them.

They had a long established social order. The men married at about 18 years and the women from 14 to 16. When a man sought a wife, he killed a deer and took it to the wikiup of his choice. Custom ordered that he enter the girl's home and pay no attention to her. If she had no interest in him, incivility would be mutual.

If the girl decided to become his bride, she watered his horse and fed it, unstrapped the deer, prepared the meat, cared for the skin, and invited her lover to eat the freshly cooked deer. They were then husband and wife.

The Utes practiced the Dog Dance, a

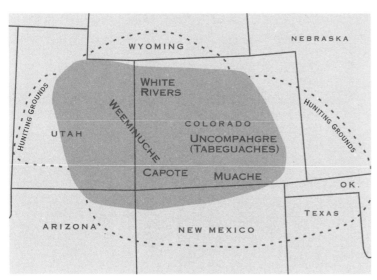

Original Ute Domain

The Remaining Ute Lands

war dance for men only. The Tea Dance was for both men and women, and was similar to the Sioux Indian Ghost Dance. The Lame Horse Dance was for women only. All dancing was done outdoors in a circular enclosure made of green boughs. The Bear Dance lasted four days. It was to assist the bears in their recovery from hibernation and provide them food. It also honored bears killed on a hunt.

Social responsibility was part of the Ute credo. When a Ute medicine man practiced his art, he staked his life on the success of his magic, which he procured from dead Indians who came to him in the guise of birds. He charged many blankets and other barter for his healing skills. If he failed, he could pay with his life.

Utes did not fear death. They held an idealized vision of an afterlife in a world of fair skies where there were great mountains, endless forests, grassy plains, fleet horses, beautiful women, strong men, and sweet rivers that would flow forever. There was no fear of a punitive God, just a paradise in which the spirits reside. A believer could not fear death, and neither could one be a coward. A warrior who showed fear would be forced to dress as a squaw for the rest of his life as permanent identification.

In the 1700s the Utes acquired horses which expanded their mobility and hunting territories while enlargng their tribal groups and pitting them in wars against invading Arapahoes, Cheyennes and Kiowa. The Utes reached the peak of their power and population by 1750, when they numbered about 8,000. They were feared warriors and respected fighters. Their slow but steady decline occurred as white Europeans moved into their territories in the mid 19th century. Land grabbing treaties forced the Utes into ever smaller parts of the state. This was the policy of the US government, so bent on rapid westward expansion that the Utes were rapidly swept from their historic lands and forced onto small, inhospitable reservations.

A number of treaties cajoled the Utes into remote reaches of Western Colorado while settlement pressures grew inexorably against them. The Meeker Massacre of 1879 turned the tide against the Utes. Nathan Meeker, a well-meaning but self-righteous bureaucrat who was bent on conforming the Utes to his Euro-American ways provoked an uprising that ended his life and those of ten White River Agency staff in a bloody mutilation.

Meeker was hated by the Utes for attempting to convert the nomadic Indians into farmers and threatening to end their traditional horse racing and gambling. One of the first victims of the massacre, he was stripped of his clothing, his mouth was filled with sugar, and a spike was hammered through his jaw and into the ground. A Ute later explained that this extreme measure was taken to silence Meeker's annoying tongue.

Meeker's death was avenged in 1881 when the Utes were forever expelled from their native lands. Otto Mears, the famed road builder, paid off Utes at $2 a head to sign a final treaty that placed them in two small reservations, one in eastern Utah, the other in equally remote southern Colorado. Both are desolate and unforgiving lands.

Ute Chief Ouray and his wife Chipeta.

Colorow and Ouray, Ute Chiefs

With increasing pressures from white settlement in the 1860s and '70s, the U.S. government recognized Ouray, translated "The Arrow," as Chief of the Ute Nation (as the seven bands of Utes were collectively called). The Utes themselves did not recognize a central leader who could speak for all, each group having its own leader. Otto Mears was the catalyst who recognized Ouray's skill at compromise and put it to good use. Ouray's father was an Uncompahgre, his mother a Jicarilla Apache. He was born in 1836 at Taos, New Mexico and as a boy worked as a sheep herder for Mexican ranchers. Here he learned the languages and customs of the Americans. When time came for a diplomat to deal with the Whites, Ouray was well-suited.

Amiable and honest, Ouray was highly regarded. He was conciliatory and realized the futility of resistance, particularly after he was honored with a visit to Washington, DC, and saw the vast numbers of white Americans with their cities, troops and machines. He joined his white mentors such as Mears to promote a policy of "guarded cooperation" as the only means of coping with the insatiable demands and overwhelming numbers of white settlers. Ouray's methods were not appreciated by all Utes, however, and there were several factions that warred constantly with Whites. Foremost among them was the sub-chief Colorow.

Colorow was born an Arapaho and captured by a Ute war party when he was a child. Raised by the Utes, Colorow soon accepted their ways and became loyal to his adoptive people. He won his status as a warrior in a battle against a large band of Arapaho warriors on Red Hill, just north of Carbondale.

As a young man Colorow married a maiden. Like him, she was also born an Arapaho, taken captive, and raised since childhood by the Utes. To his great sorrow, she died during child birth. Colorow left her remains somewhere in the Crystal Valley. Every summer he presented an armload of columbines to her memory.

In 1878 when Colorow had become a sub chief of the Utes and bore the reputation of a mighty warrior, he witnessed the flood of white settlers into the Crystal Valley with a heavy heart and a warrior's spirit. When yet another treaty threatened Ute autonomy, Colorow

COLORADO HISTORICAL SOCIETY

Ute sub chief Colorow.

reportedly broke his lance across his knee in defiance, vowing to fight for his beloved homeland.

Colorow raided farms and ranches, set forest and brush fires and helped lead the attack on troops coming to the rescue of White River Agent Nathan Meeker in 1879. When the Utes were finally pushed out of Colorado in 1881, a year after Ouray's death, Colorow still wouldn't capitulate. He gathered a band of warriors and led raids from the Utah reservation. He also returned to the Crystal Valley every autumn to hunt in his old stomping grounds.

For four years the U.S. Cavalry sent a contingent of soldiers to round up Colorow and escort him back to the reservation. Because of the expense of this military venture, and because it was ineffective in deterring this headstrong Ute, the effort was abandoned. Colorow

JOHN MCEVOY

The Dominguez-Escalante Expedition sign marker between Paonia and Hotchkiss commemorating the incredible journey.

Dominguez and Escalante - 1776

The first contact between the Ute Indians and white Europeans occurred early in the 1700s when the Ute's traded captive slaves with the Spaniards in New Mexico. By 1750, a formal treaty allowed free travel to Spaniards in Ute territories. The first formal expedition was led by Juan de Rivera, from 1761 to 1765. De Rivera made three trips into Colorado, traveling as far north as Delta on the Gunnison River.

In 1776, the Spanish government in New Mexico decided a new route to the missions of California was needed and sent two Franciscan emissaries, Fray Silvestre Velez de Escalante and Fray Francisco Atanasio Dominguez. They became the first recorded Europeans to see the Upper Grand Valley of the Colorado.

During their expedition through present day Colorado, they traveled a portion of the West Elk Loop in the North Fork Valley, following the North Fork of the Gunnison River through current day Hotchkiss, Paonia and Bowie. They then went up one of the many creeks to Grand Mesa (called Thunder Mountain by the Indians), probably Hubbard Creek. to the edge of the Muddy District. Near the present site of the Electric Mountain Lodge, north of Paonia, they encountered their first Ute Indians, a sizable band. Following is an excerpt from their journal.

"On the 1st of September we set out... after going three leagues through small narrow valleys of abundant pastures and thick clumps of scrub oak we came upon 80 Yutas, all on good horses... As soon as we halted, Padre Fray Francisco

Atanasio went... to see the chieftain... and asked him to gather there the people on hand. He did so, and when those of either sex who could attend had been assembled, he announced the Gospel through the interpreter."

The friars made an incredible journey that took them 1,000 miles through rugged mountains and often dry, barren desert. They encountered bearded Indians and experienced many trials and hardships. Their 15-member expedition traveled from July 1776 to January 1777, but failed to reach Monterey. They eventually turned back toward Taos from north central Utah, discouraged by the huge distances of the West.

The Spaniards were followed on their westward journey by fur trappers and mountain men, prospectors and traders.

Then came the American explorers: Zebulon Pike (1804), John C. Fremont (1843), John Gunnison (1853), Richard Sopris (1860), John Wesley Powell (1868) and the Ferdinand Hayden Survey (1873).

The Newcomers

Mineral wealth and seemingly unbounded natural resources became the stuff of legend and inspired a surge of westward settlement that neither Rocky Mountains, grizzly bears, severe winters nor Ute raiding parties could deter. The prime motivations were acquisition and empire. Human enterprise became a force that knew no bounds. The age of exploration became the age of exploitation, and the territory defined by the West Elk Loop was born in boom towns, mining strikes, farms and ranches, toll roads, railroads, violence, greed, cheap land, hopes and dreams....

was allowed to make his annual migration. Hunting, however, was not Colorow's only interest in the Crystal. The valley held the cherished memory of his beloved and he visited her until he was too old to make the long journey.

Backpackers in the upper Crystal, when awakened to the light of a full moon illuminating Colorow's sacred "shining mountains," claim to have seen the ethereal form of an Indian brave floating through the aspen groves. The apparition carries a bow and a quiver of arrows across his back. He wears a long-fringed buckskin shirt, and his arms cradles a bouquet of columbines.

SECTION 1

The Crystal Valley

Mount Sopris has watched over the Crystal River Valley for eons. The Utes camped on these bluffs but by 1905 no trace of them remained. Carbondale had grown to a thriving farming and railroad town.

The First People

Little remains of the first residents of the Crystal Valley - the Ute Indians. Old timers claim a stone barricade on the crest of Red Hill, just north of Carbondale, once served as a Ute fortification during a battle with marauding Arapahos. In the early days of white settlement colored beads and arrowheads were found on Red Hill and poles held horizontally by the branches of pinon and juniper trees indicated burial litters for braves.

The Utes held the Crystal and lower Roaring Fork valleys until 1881, when they were expelled to Utah on the fateful "trip of sorrows." Before then the Utes had spent countless summers hunting and fishing in 7,000 square miles of prime hunting grounds. They regarded the Yampa Hot Springs at today's Glenwood Springs as a sacred place of healing and they wintered at Antler's, a camp between Rifle and Silt, along the Colorado River.

The Utes also soaked and rested in the Penny Hot Springs on the Crystal River, where they established an encampment on their migrations to their favorite bear and elk hunting grounds in the Muddy Divide area, reached by an old trail over McClure Pass. It was trails like those that the first explorers followed through Western Colorado.

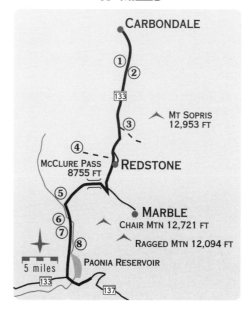

THE CRYSTAL VALLEY
47 MILES

CARBONDALE

133

Mt Sopris
12,953 FT

McClure Pass
8755 FT

REDSTONE

MARBLE
Chair Mtn 12,721 FT

Ragged Mtn 12,094 FT

Paonia Reservoir

5 miles

133

137

1. **Fish Hatchery, mile 65**
2. **Mt sopris turnouts, mile 64**
3. **Avalanche Creek, mile 54**
4. **Coal Creek, mile 50**
5. **The Muddy Creek, mile 40**
6. **Chair Mountain view, mile 38**
7. **Ragged Mountain view, mile 34**
8. **Mud slide area, mile 28**

In August 1919 a lost DeHaviland bi-plane landed at Big Four Ranch near Carbondale. The pilot was Lt. Nutt! It was the first airplane to land at Carbondale and the pilot landed when he couldn't find Glenwood Springs.

Carbondale

The first white man credited to have explored the town site of Carbondale was William Gant, a prospector who traveled the region during the Colorado gold rush of 1859. Gant reported finding an old rusted pan that indicated an even earlier visit, possibly from a "Forty-Niner" en route to California.

The first official explorer in the region was Richard Sopris, for whom the landmark peak, Mt. Sopris (12,953 ft.), is named. Born in 1813 in Bucks County, Pennsylvania, Sopris had worked as a canal contractor, a steamboat captain on the Ohio River, and a railroad contractor. He came to Colorado during the gold rush of 1859 and first mined along the Platte River near Denver. He was elected president of a miner's union local and later won a seat in the Legislature representing Arapahoe County, Territory of Kansas.

In 1860 Captain Sopris organized an expedition of gold-seekers to explore west into the mountains. They left Denver and traversed South Park, passed the present site of Breckenridge, followed the Blue River, the Eagle River, and finally entered the Roaring Fork Valley where they camped at the base of Sopris Peak. The expedition went north to Glenwood Springs then looped south to Cochetopa Pass near Gunnison. They traversed the San Luis Valley and returned to Denver three months after having set out. Captain Sopris was elected Mayor of Denver in 1879. He died there in 1893. The Sopris party reported finding no gold in the Crystal Valley.

The next known visitors to the Crystal Valley had a rather short stay. Benjamin Graham and six companions built a small fort-like cabin close to the headwaters of the Crystal near Schofield Park in 1870 to serve as a base while prospecting for gold. They were chased out by Utes who burned their cabin. Next came Ferdinand Hayden of the U.S. Geological Survey who passed through in 1873-74, mapping extensively and bringing back the first pictures of the area by the legendary photographer William Henry Jackson.

Because the last negotiated north-south boundary of the Ute reservation bisected the Roaring Fork Valley at Carbondale, the area was officially off limits. Still, drawn by adventure and open land, "Sooners" ventured beyond the boundary.

William Dinkel, Carbondale pioneer.

One of these was William Dinkel, Carbondale's founding father.

Dinkel was a Virginia gentleman who left a comfortable plantation life at age 30, drawn west by the lure of gold and adventure. Upon reaching Buena Vista in the Arkansas Valley in the spring of 1881 he learned of a shortage of flour in the new mining camp of Aspen. He bought 800 pounds and with a partner, Robert Zimmerman, jack-packed their load over Cottonwood and Taylor Passes.

"It was difficult footing on the steep grade through deep snow," reported Dinkel. "The weather was intensely cold. We were within 200 feet of the top when one of the mules fell down. Owing to the hazardous position on the edge of the precipice, there was nothing that could be done except cut the harness. The poor beast slipped over the edge...half a mile below. We stood aghast at the sight.. For two miles we waded, sometimes knee deep, in mud and slush. It was all we could do to lift our feet and drag them along. A sorry sight we made, trudging into Aspen."

The men sold their flour at a large profit and continued down the Roaring Fork to present day Carbondale where Dinkel took note of the open valley. The men were intent on reaching Montana so they continued downvalley and spent a soothing day in the Yampa Hot Springs in current day Glenwood Springs. When they ventured north onto the Flattops they were relieved of all their possessions by hostile Utes and forced back.

Dinkel settled in Carbondale in August 1881, one month before the Utes were removed. Already several choice farms had been taken up by E. F. Prince and Myron Thompson, for whom Prince and Thompson Creeks are named.

A rough stage road built by Aspen silver magnate Jerome B. Wheeler soon connected Carbondale to Aspen. It passed by Dinkel's place, which became a stage station and store. With booming silver mining in Aspen and coal development in the hills south and west of Carbondale the road was improved and became Carbondale's Main Street. By 1883, 20 families had settled. By 1887 two railroads, the Denver & Rio Grande and the Colorado Midland, hauled freight and passengers through Carbondale.

In 1886, the Crystal River Toll Company built a road along the Crystal River toward Redstone. The road was headed toward Crystal City but didn't quite reach its goal until 1907. In 1892 the Crystal River Railway Company was incorporated and in 1893 pushed rails as far as Avalanche Creek and the community of Janeway. The train reached Redstone in 1898 where it collected John Osgood's coal and coke under the name Crystal River Railroad. The destination for the Redstone loads was Pueblo and the steel mill developed there by Osgood. By 1906 the tracks reached Marble to haul the marble quarried and finished by the Colorado-Yule Marble Company until the quarry closed in 1941. The tracks were pulled in 1942.

The arrival of the railroads spurred the Carbondale Town and Land Company to plat the town and sell lots. The settlement was first named Satank, or at one time Yellow Dog.

It was moved east to the rail terminus near Dinkel's place and named Carbondale after a Pennsylvania town and because of the presence of coal. In 1887 Carbondale had a population of 400, and in 1888 the town was officially founded as a municipality with a bank and commercial interests, including a drug store, butcher shop, livery stable, jewelry store, barber shop, blacksmith shop, a hotel, churches and 13 saloons.

Early Carbondale had its share of Old West sagas. In 1887 two trackmen, Hayden and O'Connor, quarreled and Hayden shot and killed O'Connor. In

1892 John C. Morris and Frank Chatham, local ranchers, quarreled over land ownership. A few days later they met and Morris struck Chatham "a fierce blow to Chathams' head with his six-shooter." Chatham cursed Morris's mother and fought back. Morris shot Chatham in the stomach.

While mortally wounded and "holding his bleeding insides in," Chatham drew his gun and shot Morris three times in the face. Both men died.

Thomas McClure, who immigrated to the U.S. from Ireland at 21, mined gold in Gilpin County and Leadville in 1871-76. He moved to Catherine's Store east of Carbondale in 1882. There he took up farming and grew the Red Early Rose Potato which later became the "Red McClure Potato". This potato was served at the Waldorf in New York and on ocean liners. It is a favored potato even today.

While mining provided the initial lure for many of Carbondale's early settlers, agriculture provided staying power. Carbondale's mining activity eventually fell off to be revived only sporadically, and a labor shortage severely curtailed potato growing.

Since the 1950s, Carbondale's economy has relied on Colorado Rocky Mountain School, Colorado Mountain College, cattle ranching, some coal mining, and tourism. Carbondale became a bedroom community for Aspen but has come to stand on its own as a golf and outdoor recreation area.

There was no stronger, more effective advocate for farming and ranching in the Carbondale area than Eugene Grubb.

Potato Bill with a burro string loaded with gold ore on Carbondale's Main Street. Tom Kinney reported the gold, from the Avalanche Creek area, assayed out as some of the richest in Colorado.

Eugene Grubb - Carbondale's Potato King

Born in 1850 to a prosperous, devout Pennsylvania Dutch family whose home served as a way station on the underground railroad for fugitive slaves. Grubb went to work at age 11 to help support the family while his father volunteered for the Union Army and fought in the Civil War.

His father survived the war and in 1866 took his family to Minnesota where Eugene worked as a day laborer in freighting and farming. In 1870-71 he landed a job on a Mississippi steamboat where he rose from deck hand to fireman to mate. Later, he apprenticed to a blacksmith and plow maker at $4 a month. In

1874 he married Isadora White, a school teacher, and they had four children.

Eugene followed his younger brother Lloyd to the west where Lloyd had a mining claim on Aspen Mountain. Eugene nearly froze to death and almost lost both feet from frostbite walking over Independence Pass from Leadville on frozen spring snow at night. Isadora and their first child joined him the following summer and for a year lived on Aspen Mountain while Eugene and Lloyd worked their claim.

When the claim failed to bring much reward Eugene moved into Aspen, where he opened a blacksmith shop and built a

Eugene Grubb, his potatoes, and Mount Sopris in the background.

DENVER PUBLIC LIBRARY

The Grubb Ranch south of Carbondale was renowned as a state-of-the-art farming operation, with potatoes as the big cash crop.

home. He and Lloyd made several hunting trips down the Roaring Fork Valley to the vicinity of Carbondale which Eugene immediately loved. In 1885 Eugene drove a lame mule and buggy to Carbondale intent on buying a ranch.

The site he favored - at the location of the Crystal River Fish Hatchery just south of town on State Highway 133 - was already owned by three men whom he quickly discovered were quarreling. With his engaging personality Eugene sympathized with each man and won their trust. He charmed one man into trading his claim for the buggy. Another gave up his

right for the lame mule. The third sold him an option for $1.

Returning to Aspen Eugene convinced a successful miner who had also acquired a ranch in the valley that he needed brood mares and should stake Eugene on a buying trip to Illinois. The man agreed and Eugene returned with his client's horses and several of his own, including a stallion, "Centennial", and a running mare, "Katie". Grubb traded his Aspen blacksmith shop for five cows and with Lloyd moved his family to Carbondale.

The Grubb brothers cleared their land, plowed and planted 20 acres of oats, wheat and garden truck, and built three and a half miles of irrigation ditch.

Eugene erected a blacksmith shop and used his blacksmithing as barter for horse teams and plowing done by other ranchers.

His stallion was the only stud in the region and brought in good money for service fees. His mare raced at the local track, where she earned Eugene a tidy sum on wagers. Eugene continued importing brood mares from the East and soon had built himself an excellent reputation plus a sizable herd of short horn cattle.

Eugene continually expanded his land holdings until Lloyd, who was more conservative, disapproved. Eugene then bought out his brother and continued building up his ranch. By the late 1800s he had his own slaughtering plant where he sold dressed beef. He had also taken up potato cultivation, which would become a lifelong passion.

Grubb's 1,800-acre ranch was fully stocked and equipped with a shop, potato cellar, irrigation system, concrete cold

Planting potatoes was hard work for all.

It is show time at Potato Day, with fine draft horses competing for the 1912 honors.

POTATO DAY

Potato Day has been an ongoing October celebration in Carbondale since 1909. At first the celebration was free and featured roasted meat and cream-style potatoes in the skin, all prepared by area ranchers and farmers.

Starting Friday night an oak fire heated a huge barbecue pit. Beef was seasoned with sauce and wrapped in cloth, burlap and poultry wire, and when the heat was just right the meat was dumped into the hot coals. The pit was covered with iron doors and eight inches of soil, so any seeping smoke betrayed a flaw in the air-tight seal needed for a good barbecue. Eighteen hours later the beef was cooked to delectable tenderness and ready for the celebration supper.

Like a county fair, Potato Day featured contests for other locally grown produce. Field grasses, baked goods, and needle work were also judged, and there were horse and pony races, sack races and a greased pig chase. When potato fields still bordered town a contest was held to see who could pick the most potatoes in a certain time. In later years a rodeo was added to the events.

Potato varieties grown in Carbondale included Russet Burbank, White Peachblow, Gold Coin, Peoples, Red Peachblow, Red McClure, Russet Rural, White Cobblers, Red Pontiac and Bliss Triumph. Today, despite a lack of commercial potato crops, Potato Day has a parade and town-wide celebrations, honoring Carbondale's heritage. A few potatoes are grown for personal use.

storage and a rail loading station. His home had electric lights and city water. A carload of shorthorn range steers from his Mt. Sopris Farm won the championships and sweepstakes over all ages and breeds at the 1904 St. Louis World's Fair, then a championship at the International Live Stock Exposition in Chicago.

In 1901, Grubb had traveled through Europe to study agriculture. He was impressed by potato cultivation techniques in England, many of which he adapted at his Carbondale farm. Grubb became a consulting agriculturalist and was commissioned by the U. S. Secretary of Agriculture to write a definitive book describing potato cultivation all over the world. This tome was published in 1915 and became the standard text on the subject.

It was reported that on his many trips to Europe, his "engaging and magnetic personality" helped him find his way into the house of a tenant farmer and the castle of the land proprietor with equal facility. Everywhere he made friends and everywhere he acquired information that was invaluable to him.

The Bar-Forks Ranch barn serves today as the center of activities at Colorado Rocky Mountain School.

Colorado Rocky Mountain School

Founded in 1953 by John and Anne Holden, teachers from the Putney School of Vermont, the Colorado Rocky Mountain School campus spreads over the old Bar-Forks Ranch just west of Highway 133 one mile south of Highway 82. The ranch, noted for its huge, historic barn, was originally owned by Captain Isaac Cooper, a pioneer of the Roaring Fork Valley. The barn was built on the pattern of ones he had seen in Siam - the only such barn in the mountain region! Cooper also surveyed and founded Glenwood Springs which he named for his home town, Glenwood, Iowa. The ranch was later owned by former Aspen Mayor Harold "Shorty" Pabst, the 6'4" son of the famous brewer.

Begun as a summer session-only college prep school, the CRMS curriculum was designed as "an antidote for easy, modern living." The school (grades 9-12) offers scholastic programs with a strong thrust in service work and wilderness experience. Mountain biking and rock climbing, desert camping trips to Utah's Canyonlands, winter survival, ski programs and kayaking comprise the school's physical education. The campus ranch gives students hands-on experience with the annual hay crop and gardens. Among the school's amenities is a six forge blacksmith shop on campus led by master blacksmith Francis Whitaker.

Service work is outdoor-oriented and includes trail building in the White River National Forest. Students focus on natural resource conservation, energy efficiency, environmental science, composting, gardening, riparian habitat, and on-site language education in Mexico and Canada. Fall enrollment is limited to 165, of which 10 percent are international students.

The Crystal River Fish Hatchery

The Crystal River Hatchery has been a brood hatchery for trout since 1941. Located on the west side of Highway 133 a mile south of Carbondale, it utilizes an abundance of natural spring water. The hatchery produces 15 million eggs a year from rainbow and cutthroat trout, with eggs and semen taken from a stock of 200,000 fish.

Technicians capture the fish by stunning them with a mild electric shock. They milk the semen and eggs from males (bucks) and females (does), fertilize the eggs, allow them to harden, then ship them to hatcheries across the state where they're raised into fingerlings and later released. The hatchery boasts a 95 percent fertilization rate, compared with less than one percent in nature.

Janeway and Avalanche Creek

Leaving Carbondale, Highway 133 crosses open meadows and hay fields, then enters a narrowing canyon. Here, Hugh Pattison, a Carbondale blacksmith, prospected on Avalanche Creek in 1880 and reported a past prospect that may have been signs of the Richard Sopris party 20 years before. Though the Avalanche area is crystalline in nature and worthy of potentially rich ore, several prospecting ventures and a full-scale mining operation in 1899 failed to prove a strike.

There is an alabaster quarry operating in the summer up the Avalanche Creek road across the Crystal River.

In 1881 John Mobley moved to the junction of the Crystal and Avalanche Creek and started a small settlement. He and his wife and two children had come over Schofield Pass from Crested Butte along the headwater of the Crystal in 1880 and first established a home near Marble.

On the trip over Schofield Pass Mobley's supplies included a 50-pound sack of flour, one bar of soap, a box of matches, but no salt. The children rode inside the panniers on a burro that spooked and ran off. The animal was finally stopped far down the trail by William Woods, a miner who in later years became known as one of Marble's founders.

After the winter of 1880 in Marble, where the pack animals had to browse on willows, the Mobley children, Nellie and Chet, found their way up Carbonate Creek to the cabin of miners William D. Parry and G. D. Griffith. The children begged salt and, to the astonishment of the miners gulped it down like candy.

The Mobleys moved from Marble to Avalanche and established Mobley's Camp, later named Janeway after Mary Jane Francis, a wealthy, adventursome woman who traveled to the area on horseback to look over mining claims she had acquired. The claims proved worthless but Mary Jane fell in love with the Crystal Valley and made it her home.

FRANCIS WHITAKER MASTER BLACKSMITH

A wrist brace the color of coal dust and reinforced with a steel bar tells of more than six decades that Francis Whitaker, artist blacksmith, has been pounding hot steel on an anvil. Now past age 90 Whitaker is widely revered by fellow blacksmiths as being "the source" for an ancient, resurgent art.

In his book, "Recipes in Iron," Whitaker describes in cookbook fashion many of his creations. This guide to blacksmiths has inspired many at the Colorado Rocky Mountain School Campus of Carbondale, where Whitaker holds master classes.

Francis Whitaker, master blacksmith.

As a young man, Whitaker began learning his craft from Samuel Yellin of Philadelphia whom Whitaker regards as "the greatest iron worker of this century." He later worked with an equally fine master, Julius Schramm of Berlin. "The first time I got a piece of iron hot and set it on the anvil and started to hammer it, I was hooked," says Whitaker. "It's magical - a combination of metal, earth, fire and water."

Following his apprenticeship Whitaker lived in Carmel, California from the late 1920s through the '60s. He moved to Aspen where his Mountain Forge produced blacksmith artwork for 25 years. He has been on the CRMS campus the past eight years and shows no sign of tiring. He is as tough and resilient as the steel he hammers and credits his excellent health to an active life as a runner, skier, and hiker.

In 1997 Whitaker received a National Endowment for the Arts award for his blacksmithing acumen. While honorariums abound one stands out on the wall of the CRMS blacksmith shop, above the desk where Whitaker works. It reads: "To the master, Francis Whitaker, with sincere thanks. His students." That plaque may be the most important recognition of all.

She lived on the south end of Carbondale and became a well-loved benefactress of the town. She was widely recognized as she sped by in her shiny spring wagon with a uniformed coachman driving a beautiful team of matched black horses.

Mobley secured a post office under the name Janeway in 1887, and a year later the settlement had a population of 50 but the post office had been moved to Redstone. Janeway became a station on the Crystal River Railroad.

Transportation problems were different in the old days of the Crystal Valley.

CAROL CRAVEN PHOTO

A big horn ram jumps free of captors near Avalanche Creek in the Crystal River Valley where a large herd inhabits the rocky crags and is often seen by motorists. Some of the herd was relocated to invigorate the health of other herds.

At the turn of the century an early resident of Janeway, Ed Gift, was visited by a game warden who discovered a haunch of poached deer in Gift's cabin. Gift was arrested and he and the evidence were taken by wagon to Aspen. The trip was long so the warden and the suspect stayed overnight in Carbondale. The wagon was put up at Hugh Pattison's shop.

Pattison was a friend of Gift's and in the night he took the deer haunch down to the local butcher shop and matched it as closely as he could with a veal haunch, swapping the two. Secretly, he advised Ed to claim, at the trial, that the haunch was not poached deer, but veal, which Ed did. Men were called to examine the haunch and they verified Ed's claim, to the chagrin of the warden.

Back in Carbondale Ed Gift hunted up Pattison and asked what became of the venison haunch. Pattison laughed and rubbed his tummy. "What do you suppose, Ed, what do you suppose?"

The Crystal Valley Railway reached Janeway in 1893, the year of the great Silver Panic. Following the decline of mining fortunes in the Crystal Valley the town faded away. All that remains is a weathered log cabin, once the stage station, which can be seen across the river from the White River National Forest sign.

Avalanche Creek is a trailhead to Avalanche Lake and Buckskin Basin in the Maroon Bells-Snowmass Wilderness Area. The US Forest Service Avalanche Campground is three miles up the dirt road from Highway 133.

Penny Hot Springs

Penny Hot Springs is marked by a turnout on the east side of Highway 133, just above "the narrows", a granite section of the canyon cut by the Crystal River. The springs are named for Dan Penny who kept a small hotel on the railroad line upstream of Avalanche Creek. Penny's guests would stay at his hotel and use the hot springs bathhouse–one side for men, the other for women.

The tubs were marble, but the divider in the bathhouse only extended to the water surface, so bathing attire was prudent for all enjoying the hot water.

The spring remained popular but obscure until the 1960s when young people began to bathe there *au natural*. Nearby residents, offended by nudity and other unseemly acts, bulldozed the bathhouse and attempted to destroy the springs - once pouring tar into the pools, another time dumping large boulders into them. But there was no stopping the

MARBLE BALLAST

While traveling along the Crystal River one sees evidence of marble quarried in the upper valley until about 1940. The old right-of-way of the Crystal River Railroad (still visible today) is shored up with white chunks of Marble along the river side. These trimming and rejects were dumped along the route to provide ballast against the constant erosion of the Crystal River.

That they remain today for travelers to ponder is because they are simply too heavy to cart off!

geothermal activity and there was no stopping a cadre of local hot springs enthusiasts who rebuilt the pools and fought to make them public. In the early 1990s Pitkin County acquired the property and made the springs officially public. Swim suits are officially required.

Redstone

Regarded as a coal miner's utopia the town of Redstone was a rare example of social engineering and aesthetic planning. Compared to the abysmal conditions in most American coal mining camps, which were plagued by low wages, corporate domination, lack of sanitation and typhoid fever, Redstone shone like a gem and felt like a resort.

The reason was the desire of coal mining king John C. Osgood and his associate J. A. Kebler to improve the lot of their 16,000 employees. After having quelled four strikes against his company the

The Colorado Supply Company Store in Redstone, 1905. The Company Store was standard for John Osgood's Colorado Fuel & Iron Company camps and plants to provide for the needs of the isolated workers. Most were not so elegant as the Redstone store.

American way, by hiring strike breakers and permitting violence, in 1901 Osgood and Kebler appointed Dr. Richard Corwin as head of Colorado Fuel and Iron's new "Sociological Department." Corwin had been head of the company's hospital in Pueblo and was a pioneer in the new science of sociology.

Osgood had already begun construction at Redstone for his model village, but when given his charter Corwin launched an ambitious program of social uplift for all 38 of the company's coal camps, rolling mills and steel works in Colorado, Wyoming and New Mexico. The program affected both the workers

and their 60,000 family members. New houses were built, including a clubhouse for miners at each camp, kindergartens, night schools and libraries. Classes were offered in sewing, cooking and hygiene. A company magazine, *Camp and Plant*, was distributed, with articles on health and hygiene, nutrition, child care, education and healthful recreation. Included were regular news reports on social and cultural activities from each camp so that the scattered employees could feel that they were part of the company.

Osgood's first Colorado ranch was not far from Redstone, so in the late 1880s it was easy for him to start his great invest-

The Redstone Inn was built by coal king John Osgood to house his bachelor coal miners. Architecturally, the Inn set the tone for one of the finest coal company towns in the west.

Horseback riders along the Crystal River near Redstone.

ment in making Redstone a state-of-the-art company town. His own summer home was to be built just a mile upstream, and he already had ranches there. He employed famous architects to design 88 cottages and homes for workers and foremen so that no two were alike.

The cottages, some of which are still in use, had electricity, running water, plaster and lath interiors with wall covering, matching outbuildings, bright colors, grassy yards, fences, garden plots and tree-shaded streets. Redstone got its electricity from the Osgood hydroelectric plant and a reservoir above town provided water piped into all homes by cast iron water mains. There were fire hydrants and a fire station.

For his bachelor employees Osgood

built an elegant frame and sandstone inn with 14 bedrooms, electric lights, a barbershop, laundry, telephones, reading rooms and steam heat. This is now the 35 room Redstone Inn, which stands as a handsome historic hotel and restaurant. Altogether, Osgood's investment in Redstone was estimated at over $300,000, a major fortune at the time.

A modern bath house was built and it was a rule that workers were not to appear on public streets after their shifts until they had bathed and changed clothes. The Redstone Club offered all the modern refinements of the day-bar, lounge, reading and game rooms, and a theater with dressing rooms, scenery and an arc-illuminated stereopticon.

Camp and Plant reported that, in an

effort toward temperance, the bar "will sell to members or visitors wines, beers and liquors, but in order to promote their temperate use and believing that each member or visitor has the intelligence and ability to buy what he wants when he wants it without suggestion or aid from anyone, no 'treating' will be allowed".You could drink all you could afford, but you could not help anyone else get drunk!

Women were not allowed as members, but they could visit on certain evenings for whist and euchre parties, billiards, pool and light refreshments, which "together with instrumental music, combine to make these evenings pass away all too quickly."

Osgood's improvements were completed by 1902, at which time Redtone's 249 beehive coke ovens, operational since 1899, produced 11,000 tons of high grade coke a month. It was shipped by rail to the Pueblo steel mill.

Coalbasin employed 296 miners, who mined 800 tons of coal per day. Coal was brought to the surface by mule power, then loaded on the narrow gauge "High Line" railroad that traversed 12 miles of track to go the 8 miles down to Redstone. By the time the mines were closed and Coalbasin abandoned in 1909 over one million tons of coal had been mined.

John C. Osgood the Fuel King

The father of Redstone, John C. Osgood, was recognized during his day as one of the six most prominent captains of industry in the U.S. His family stock was colonial and revolutionary. The Andover Osgoods traced their lineage to the first Osgood pilgrim who founded the town of Andover, Massachusetts in 1627. His Cleveland ancestors settled Salisbury and Thompson in the same state at the same time. Daniel Larned, his great-grandfather, was a brigadier general in the Continental Army. Samuel Osgood, another great-grandfather, served as the country's first postmaster general under President George Washington.

Born in 1851 in Brooklyn to Samuel Warburton Osgood and Mary Hill Cleveland Osgood, John was orphaned at nine. He was taken in by relatives and sent to a Quaker school, which he left before he was 15. He started work as an office boy in New York and by 16 had obtained a clerking job. He attended night

John Cleveland Osgood

SYLVIA RULAND COLLECTION

school at Peter Cooper Institute, then known as "the poor man's Harvard."

By age 19 Osgood had moved up to the position of bookkeeper with the Union Coal & Mining Company of Burlington, Iowa and became a quick student of the coal business. By age 30 he had acquired a major interest in the Whitebreast Coal and Mining Company in Ottumwa, Iowa which supplied fuel to the Chicago, Burlington and Quincy Railroad. He came west in 1882 to explore Colorado's coal

reserves for that railroad and himself.

On that visit he surveyed the Crystal River Valley. He chanced upon W. D. Parry and G. D. Griffith, a pair of gold miners who had just escaped with their lives from an avalanche that swept through their camp on Coal Creek. To the disappointment of the gold seekers the slide had uncovered only a large coal deposit. Osgood bought their claim for $500 and so began an odyssey of land acquisitions in the Crystal Valley that lasted his lifetime.

Osgood got financial backing from Denver and Iowa investors. He formed the Colorado Fuel Company with partner J. A. Kebler, a graduate of the Massachusetts School of Technology with a degree in mining engineering. Within a decade the wheeling, dealing Osgood had bought up promising mines and all the coal he could from mines he didn't own, becoming sole supplier to some regional railroads and furnishing high quality coking coal to precious metal smelters across the Rockies.

In the early 1890s Osgood and his chief competitor, the Pueblo-based Colorado Coal and Iron Company, merged. The Colorado Fuel & Iron Company - CF&I - became the industrial giant of the west, controlling vast coal reserves estimated at 400 million tons. CF&I owned 14 coal mines, 800 coke ovens, iron mines and the only integrated Bessemer steel plant in the West, located in Pueblo. Osgood became CF&I's president and later board chairman, responsible for rapid expansion of the company. He raised $40 million for the expansion in the ten years he headed the enterprise.

The CF&I merger was a clash of titans.

Alma Osgood in 1906 driving her 1904 Pope-Winton electric car at Cleveholm Manor.

School children and their teacher, Norma Kinney, at Redsdtone, 1922.

Alma Osgood's Brewster wicker carriage in the courtyard of the Redstone Castle.

Osgood took over the steel company founded by the visionary General William Jackson Palmer, who earlier had organized the Denver and Rio Grande Railway and the city of Colorado Springs. A big factor in the takeover was that investors knew Palmer paid no dividends while Osgood was always profitable and always paid a large return to investors.

One of Osgood's early acts was building 21 miles of standard gauge track between Carbondale and Placita in the Crystal River Valley, although because of the 1893 silver crash and ensuing depression, it was not completed until 1898.

Though he traveled a great deal, had a city block home in New York City, leased an estate in England for six months out of each year, and had homes in Denver and Pueblo, Osgood considered Redstone his special home, one on which he could lavish attention as if it were an only child.

His first wife, Irene, set Glenwood Springs ablaze with her Bohemian flare. Irene was 22, beautiful, unconventional and of uncertain origin. She wrote "romantic" fiction which passed for pornography in those days and her husband established a publishing firm which produced her first novel, *A Shadow of Desire*. The New York Times panned the book as "unredeemed by any particle of common sense ... as unwholesome as any we have had the bad fortune to read."

The couple divorced in 1898. A year later Osgood came to Redstone with another bride, Alma Regina Shelgrem. Reputed to be a Swedish Countess, Alma was an excellent horsewoman and pianist, intelligent and well-educated. It was for Alma that Osgood built Cleveholm

Manor, today known as the Redstone Castle. She was heralded as "Lady Bountiful" for her acts of generosity and kindness to the workers and their families, particularly the children.

While Redstone flourished with Osgood's beneficence, the future was full of doubt. In 1902 Chicago financier and barbed wire king John W. "Bet a Million" Gates acquired a large interest in CF&I and fought to win control of the company.

Buffalo Bill with King Leopold of Belgium. Leopold was a guest of John Osgood at Cleveholm Manor.

The remains of the coke ovens line the byway route across Highway 133 from Redstone, a National Historic District. Redstone has a historical museum and public park, unusual for a town with population 92.

Osgood won the battle but at exorbitant expense. The next year another takeover was attempted by George Gould, Edwin Hawley and E. H. Harriman. By 1903 CF&I was nearly insolvent. To save the company, Osgood relinquished control to John D. Rockefeller who had backed him in the takeover fights. Colorado's biggest industry became owned and managed by eastern interests.

Rockefeller urged Osgood to remain as chairman, but the independent leader would have none of it. He left the company and by 1911 he had left Redstone. He kept his beloved Cleveholm Manor, which was mothballed and to which he didn't return for many years. CF&I retained control of Coalbasin and Osgood quickly reestablished himself as an industrial leader with the Victor-American Fuel Company which he headed as president and chairman of the board.

After Osgood left CF&I the hard won social programs he endorsed were slowly scrapped. In 1903, the year Osgood left, miners in nine CF&I camps walked out in sympathy with striking coal miners in the east, infuriating management.

By the time of the coal field wars of 1913-14, marked by the tragedy of the Ludlow Massacre, Osgood had retained his business acumen, but as spokesman for the coal operators he had little charity toward labor or unions. The American way of that day had management always right, regardless of the issues.

Osgood and Alma divorced in 1912 and Osgood disappeared for 10 years, finally returning to Redstone in 1925 with his third wife. She was 30, he was 74. He died of abdominal cancer and the consequences of botched surgery in January 1926 and left his entire estate, worth over $4.5 million, to Lucille, his wife of six years.

She received cash, the Victor American Fuel Company, the New York and other homes, many investments in stock, and of course his beloved Crystal Valley, about 19,000 acres from Marble to Carbondale. Osgood's ashes were scattered in the Crystal Valley.

"MANSION" AT REDSTONE, COLO.

The Osgood estate - Cleveholm Manor - at Redstone was built on a baronial scale reflecting the elegance, taste and style of John Osgood, one of the major industrialists of his time.

Cleveholm: The Redstone Castle

Originally named Cleveholm Manor (*Cleve's home* in Swedish), the Redstone Castle is a baronial structure completed in 1902. Architect to the rich Theodore Davis Boal designed the mansion on 4,200 acres of fenced land straddling the Crystal River. The mansion has 42 rooms and offers a dramatic statement about the exalted status of its owner and lord, John Osgood.

After all, while his contemporaries were showing off in Newport and the Hamptons, he built his summer home in the Colorado wilderness, reached by his own railroad!

Woodwork was of the finest mahogany or oak paneling. Many other rooms and hallways were decorated by skilled artists.

Their stenciling and other detail added a patina of richness to the already impressive structure. Polished hardwood floors were covered by priceless Oriental carpets. The vast fireplaces, the main one bearing the Osgood crest cut in stone, and the massive furnishings were outstanding examples of the finest in stone and woodwork created by master craftsmen.

The library and dining rooms boasted gold-leaf ceilings. Two other rooms had elegant domed ceilings. The English-style great room was lighted by three Tiffany chandeliers, hanging by brass chains from the 19-foot ceiling. Leather-bound volumes in the library blended with the warmth of leather-covered walls.

The dining room featured mahogany wainscotting topped by Russian cut velvet, Tiffany light fixtures and the gold-leaf ceiling helped highlight glistening, gracefully curved plate glass of towering, hand-carved cabinets. Those held ornate silver candle sticks, serving trays and centerpieces, and delicate Venetian glass goblets.

The approach to Cleveholm was past impressive gate houses. In the horse-drawn age carriages and broughams circled behind the mansion into the cobbled courtyard where horses could drink from a wrought iron, winged dragon fountain pouring a stream of mountain water into a horse trough cut from a single, pure white statuary grade marble block from Osgood's own quarry. Since Redstone was far from any fresh flower market, a large greenhouse was constructed by glaziers from New Jersey.

Osgood had nearby farms for domestic livestock, vegetable gardens, and special purebred horses and cattle. He also maintained a fenced elk and deer pasture on Deer Park across from his mansion, where he grew hay in the summer, fed the animals in the winter, and released all of them in the spring after the calves and fawns were born. A German gamekeeper lived adjacent to the park and made pets of some of the animals.

Deer Park now is a subdivision and the gamekeeper's cottage a private residence.

Cleveholm's construction was estimated at $500,000, with another $200,000 for furnishings. The estate had electric lights and indoor plumbing when most of New York City did not!

The Castle was used sparingly after Osgood's death and many of the outbuildings were sold by the widow to be wrecked for salvage - to get them off the property tax rolls as the Great Depression deepened. About 1940 the mansion was sold to two sisters for $10,000; World War II and its gas rationing and travel restrictions kept them in Redstone until 1944 when the mansion sold to Mr. and Mrs. H. R. Hibbert of Golden for $20,000. It was rumored that the gold leaf stripped from the ceilings paid the purchase price. Like many myths surrounding Osgood this was untrue; an attempt to reclaim this thinnest of gold decoration only resulted in costly damage to the library ceiling and no money for the effort.

The home was used for two years as a guest house and sold again in 1946 for $110,000 to C. Dean and Rose Cook of Denver. They developed it into a dude ranch, operating summers only, for the next 10 years. It was called Crystal River Lodge. Since then, various owners have operated it as an inn, open to the public for lodging and tours.

Coalbasin

At Coalbasin, eight miles west of Redstone at 9,500 feet elevation where the coal was mined, Osgood built an equally modern and attractive community. Today only foundations and a railroad bridge abutment remain of this once-thriving model company town.

The Colorado Supply Company started a store in Coalbasin in 1900 for the needs of miners. The store was an outpost surrounded by wilderness. Wild columbines grew in profusion around the store and cowboys riding herd on the nearby cattle range attested to its remote surroundings.

The Great Room of Cleveholm Manor features Tiffany chandeliers and light fixtures, a record elk above the fireplace, and the Osgood family crest.

CF&I's *Camp and Plant* publication reported the sighting of five bears and a "drove of mountain sheep" seen just above the camp where at one time 269 men were employed.

In 1905 the camp had a population of 150, a hotel, a doctor and the club house with its bar. In November 1908, following a drinking spree, Frank Buth killed Peter Niora. The body was taken to Redstone for burial and Buth was taken to trial in Aspen.

Following the mine closure in 1909 Coalbasin became a ghost town whose buildings were used occasionally by hunters. Mining resumed in the 1950s when Mid-Continent Resources reopened operations to provide coking quality coal to steel mills in Provo, Utah and Fontana, California. The mines were pocketed with dangerous methane gas. Fifteen miners died in an explosion there in 1981.

Mid-Continent trucked the coal in special 6-wheel-drive trucks down the long, steep grade to the wash plant, a task formerly handled by the narrow gauge train with its Ingoldsby patent dump cars. The cleaned coal was transferred by bigger trucks to Carbondale, where it shipped out by rail. When the two steel mills were closed by strikes in the 1980s, Mid-Continent marketed coal to Asia. Mid-Continent shut down in 1991 and Coal Basin is being reclaimed virtually back to the wild state found by John Osgood when he bought the claim over 100 years earlier.

Coalbasin school 1902; Miss Josephine Macbeth, teacher and Dr. W. E. Ashby, resident physician.

Doctor Angus Taylor was physician for both Redstone and nearby Placita, where this picture was taken.

The trestle at the Coal Basin Mine conveyed coal cars to the tipple, where coal was loaded onto a high-line train that ran 12 miles to Redstone. There, another tipple dropped the coal onto carts to be dumped into the coke ovens.

Placita

South of Redstone, Placita was the site of the old McClure Coal Tunnel. Placita was developed by Osgood's CF&I and produced 6,500 tons of coal with 35 men in 1899, when it marked the terminus of the Crystal River Railroad. In 1901 CF&I sold the mine. The post office closed in 1903. Placita remained a rail head for shipping livestock long after the railroad extended to Marble in 1906. Eugene Grubb shipped 27 car loads of cattle in 1904, and as late as 1931 the railroad delivered 210 carloads of stock, sheep and cattle to the Rio Grande at Carbondale. The rails were pulled in 1942 and Placita gradually disappeared, leaving two houses and hardly any other trace today.

McClure Pass

Before 1947 McClure Pass was little more than a rough wagon road from Placita. The Utes had used the pass as their route between the Muddy and the Crystal. "Mac" McClure built and ran a two-story hotel at nearby Bogan Flats on the Crystal River Railroad line in the early 1900s. The pass therefore became known as McClure's Pass. The old road, still easily identified by a series of switchbacks, also served for many years as a cattle trail.

John Osgood, owner of the Redstone Castle, once boasted to friends over dinner that he could drive his car to the top of the pass. This was before it had become a road. His friends made a wager that he couldn't and Osgood said he'd show them. The next day Osgood's friends ascended the pass on horseback, and there was Osgood with his car! The coal magnate had paid a group of horse freighters to disassemble his car, load it on pack animals and take it to the top of the pass, where they reassembled it.

The Muddy Region

As you rise out of the Crystal Valley and ascend McClure Pass (8,755 feet), a turnout offers a vista from Mt. Sopris and the sandstone cliffs at Redstone on the north to the rugged mountains east toward Marble. This panorama is part of the pristine, untrammeled country the first explorers found. They, and the settlers that followed, came to love this rugged beauty and called it home.

On the south side of McClure Pass, across the valley from the dramatic escarpments of Ragged Peak, lies a vast area of rolling hills and mesas called the Muddy. This little known region has remained remote and rural over many decades of western development because of its marginal value as a mining center and its distance from railroads or, in the early days, from roads of any kind.

Still, the Muddy country was traveled by migrating Ute Indians and the earliest European explorers. The Spaniards Escalante and Dominguez were probably the first white men in the area, passing through on their extensive 1776 trek via the Ute's White River trail. While the friars left journals and diaries, the early trappers, gold prospectors and mountain men who followed left only footprints and artifacts, and few of either.

The first real settlement of the Muddy was by miners in the early 1880s when horse and mule packers pushed into the region and pursued placer mining. Rotting cottonwood logs which had been hollowed out to serve as crude sluice boxes were found early in the 1900s, evidence that miners were after the fine and powdery "flour gold" found there.

The only consistent economy for the region was agriculture and the town of Ragged Mountain, located two miles west of Highway 133 at the turn-off to Collbran (near mile 38), was built by homesteaders around livestock grazing, first cattle and later sheep. A 1919 issue of the Paonian describes the new town in glowing terms: "Post office, Telephone, School and Good Roads. Vast foothill region now forging ahead rapidly to the very front ranks. The liveliest part of the county just now is the great inland empire of the Muddy district."

The "great inland empire" struggled on through lean times, and for all the boasting about good roads the area was notorious for the mud that silts appropriately

Agriculture played a major role in the Muddy district where high grasses fed cattle and farmers raised fields of grain.

named Muddy Creek. In one tale of early mail delivery, a faithful dog saved the day by delivering a distress message when the horse drawn mail coach became mired in mud up to its axles.

The mail carrier's dog, Tim, a German Shepherd, sprinted home with a note tagged to its collar. The mail carrier's father found the note, hitched a double team and went to the aid of the mail coach.

Many of the homesteaders worked winters in North Fork Valley coal mines to support their ranching and farming vocations. They also made ends meet by selling butter, milk and cream and by growing oats, barley, wheat, potatoes and hay. But cattle was the main industry, and, at times, it was big business. Claire Hotchkiss recalls the days when upwards

of 60,000 head of cattle ran on the Muddy and Grand Mesa. "I've seen the time when the road from Paonia and Hotchkiss was a continual river of cattle," she recalled.

One range boss of a big cattle operation made a deal with restaurants in Paonia and Hotchkiss to stay open around the clock to serve his many cowhands anytime they wanted a meal. The last of the big time cattle operators on the Muddy was DRC Brown, who pulled out his herds in 1926. Fluctuating cattle prices and overgrazing conspired to undermine ranching in the Muddy district, and when the Homestead Act opened public lands, much of the range was divided and fenced.

Harvest time in Western Colorado farming country meant putting up a hay crop for winter feed. Hay stackers like this were used with horse-powered mechanisms for building the huge stacks.

Laura Clock, who grew up on the Muddy, refers to the "Homestead Bug" as an affliction akin to "Gold Fever", where the number of land claims and the optimism of the claimants belied the often impossible task of making a living. "One need only observe the dilapidated ranch buildings, long deserted, many on plots of land so steep and rocky and small he marvels that anyone would have the courage or foolhardiness to claim such ground and hope to make a livelihood on it. And, of course, many of them didn't."

Many western settlements were social and financial experiments that didn't last long, and the Muddy was one. By 1956 the town of Ragged Mountain could no longer sustain a sufficient permanent population so the post office was closed. Today only scattered ranches and the old school building attest to the livelihood and the once glowing promise of the "great inland empire" called the Muddy.

The Hayrack Park Shooting

A hard-bitten rancher, Thomas Welch, came to the Muddy from Ireland in the early 1880s, staked a number of mining claims and eventually accumulated a large homestead. He raised cattle and cut wild hay with a mowing machine he had shipped by rail to Glenwood Springs and freighted by wagon to the bottom of McClure Pass. The pass was roadless then, so Welch disassembled his wagon and mower and "jackpacked" them over the pass, then reassembled them and continued on his way.

The wild hay of Hayrack Park was technically on public land but it was viewed as private domain by the Welch family for years. Finally, it drew other cattlemen who valued the hay for free summer grazing. The Welch family didn't welcome the competition.

Cowhands from the IX Ranch in the North Fork Valley notified Welch they would take their share of the natural bounty of Hayrack Park. Welch and his son, Tom, however, vowed to defend Hayrack Park, with force if necessary. They established themselves behind breastworks, armed with rifles, ready for the approach of the IX cowhands on the appointed day.

Four cowhands approached with a wagon and mower and the Welches, itchy on the trigger fingers, opened fire after declaring their intentions to defend the hay. Two cowhands riding on the wagon were killed outright and a third was wounded. A fourth cowhand, armed with a rifle, returned fire and killed Tom Welch, the son. That ended the battle of Hayrack Park. The elder Welch retreated and later packed his dead son on horseback over McClure Pass and into Carbondale for burial. The wounded cowhand died a year later.

A stanza of a poem by Laura Clock, a native of the town of Ragged Mountain, offers a eulogy to the Hayrack Park shooting and a telling chapter to the Muddy region history.

No headstones rest
On the low hill's crest
To show where the two were laid.
The only mark
Was the blaze on the bark
Of a tree, long since decayed
Fallen to earth and decayed.

The McClure Pass Mud Slide

Except for the Mount Saint Helens volcanic explosion, the McClure Pass mud slide of 1986 is the largest in the history of the United States. Its effects can be seen in fractured ground and toppled trees just before Paonia Reservoir. Rain and deep snows from high precipitation during the early 1980s saturated the ground above the pass road to the east on the lower flanks of Ragged Peak (12,641 feet), a stunning mountain 21 miles east of Paonia.

The slippage was gradual, but the whole expanse - 140 million cubic yards covering more than 1,060 acres - started down the slope at about one foot an hour and continued until it had dammed Muddy Creek and covered Highway 133. Crews worked 24 hours a day trying to keep the stream open, preventing an unstable 40-foot dam and a new lake.

Higher up on the mountain the slide reached depths of 100-150 feet. As this mass flowed, it took everything with it, including trees and the ranch home of Mrs. John Volk, a widow. The slide kept moving through May, closing the road for

Construction on Paonia Dam began in 1960 to impound water and create a silt trap to protect agricultural ditches in the North Fork Valley. The dam was completed in 1963 and has created a popular boating and fishing area.

months. It slowed to 10 feet a day by June, and by July highway crews began building a bypass 40 feet higher than the old route.

The slide, born of the Wasatch Formation (comprised of mud stones, clay stones, sand stones and sediment-formed conglomerates laid down 65 million years ago) attracted curious geologists from around the world.

Paonia Reservoir

The Colorado River Storage Project, an act passed by Congress in 1956, provided for many western reservoirs, including the Paonia Reservoir and dam. Begun in 1960 and completed in 1963 by the Bureau of Reclamation, the reservoir was built to provide flood control on Muddy Creek and act as a silt trap to clear the water before it goes into the North Fork of the Gunnison River. The water stored then feeds the Fire Mountain Canal and provides irrigation for thousands of acres of farm land and fruit orchards in the North Fork Valley. The reservoir is said to be nearly half-filled with silt from Muddy Creek, much of which came from the McClure Pass mud slide.

AT THE FOOT OF MCCLURE PASS, A TURN EAST UP THE CRYSTAL RIVER GIVES THE TRAVELER A STRONG SENSE OF THE PAST; THE MAGNIFICENT MOUNTAINS, A BEAUTIFUL VALLEY, AND CHALLENGING ROADS OPEN UP THE OLD MINING AREAS, THE MARBLE QUARRIES, AND THE REMAINS OF THE TOWNS THAT ONCE HELD WORKERS, FAMILIES, DREAMS.

The Johnson Store at Crystal City.

DENVER PUBLIC LIBRARY

Crystal City was neat and orderly, but dwarfed by the mountains. The Devil's Punchbowl and Schofield were up the Crystal River from town.

Crystal City

Long before Carbondale was settled, prospectors were swarming over the high passes from Crested Butte and Gothic into the headwaters of the Crystal Valley. Here the town of Schofield served as a jumping off point to the wilderness beyond. Long, harsh winters in Schofield and a lack of high-grade ore caused the whole town to relocate four difficult miles downstream past Crystal Canyon and the Devil's Punchbowl to what became Crystal City.

This was the camp for the Lead King Mine, a good producer whose rich ores were first packed by mule (some of them belonging to John Osgood who ran pack trains and had a fuel company in the town) through the Devil's Punchbowl and over Schofield Pass to Crested Butte. Later they went downstream to Carbondale and the railroad there.

The fortunes of Crystal declined after the silver crash of 1893. Today Crystal is a summer-only community of authentic mining-era buildings reached by a rugged 4-wheel drive road roughly six miles upstream from Marble on the Crystal River. The only year-round resident is "Lead King Paul" Harris, whose white bearded countenance and nearby rustic cabin at the old townsite of Avalanche harken to a time long ago.

The roads past Marble are gravel, then dirt, and in some places just rocky paths.

They are all considered 4-wheel-drive roads although passenger cars are seen, albeit rarely, as far as Crystal City. They are all splendid trails for mountain bicycles or horses.

The Devil's Punchbowl

Far up the Crystal River, at a point where the limpid waters become a froth of foam and rushing current, is the infamous Devil's Punchbowl. The river has carved with whatever malice it possesses a deep, narrow gorge where its funneled fury unleashes cataracts of lethal force.

A legend dating since the first intrusion of the earliest explorers tells of a man falling into this tumult and perishing deep within the punchbowl's cruel channel. He had apparently fallen from an old trail 1,000 feet above, and his remains were never found. The only evidence of such a calamity was the skeleton of a horse tethered to a tree near the trail. The story goes that the man had dismounted, secured his horse to the tree, perhaps during the first snow storm of early winter, and somehow fell to his gruesome and solitary death. The horse was left to slowly starve.

Through the years a number of travelers on the challenging road have died in four-wheel-drive accidents when their vehicles have slipped over the side and into the maelstrom.

Marble

As miners passed down the Crystal Valley, Marble was a natural stopover. Its mineral wealth was not in gold or coal, but in vast deposits of high quality marble. The marble was first surveyed and

A daring visitor perches on the marble ledge in the quarry room of the Yule Marble Quarry, giving a sense of the mammoth cavern.

claimed by Parry and Griffith in the mid 1880s on the west side of Yule Creek. Finding the marble was relatively easy, but to quarry, mill and transport it became a costly hurdle.

When coal king John Osgood built the Crystal Valley Railroad to Placita - less than eight miles from Marble - development of a quarry seemed feasible. Osgood had property interests in Marble, but his battle for control of CF&I proved a major distraction. Eastern capital finally came to Marble in 1905 when the Colorado-Yule

Marble Company was incorporated with $2.5 million. Colonel Channing Meek became its president.

Meek was an Iowan who had worked briefly as a marble cutter and railroad worker and had reached prominence as the president of the Colorado Coal & Iron Company at the time it was merging with Osgood's fuel company. Meek had collected claims and properties in Marble, and once Colorado-Yule Marble was capitalized he became heavily involved. As company president he

Loading the 56-ton block of marble destined for the Tomb of the Unknown Soldier in Arlington National Cemetery,

ambitiously expanded the quarry and constructed the finest marble finishing plant money could buy.

Meek's first contract was for $500,000 worth of marble for the new Cuyahoga County Courthouse in Cleveland, Ohio. Despite a three-month strike in 1909 by quarry workers, Meek finished the contract and had new customers in Chicago, St. Louis, New Orleans, Houston, Denver, Los Angeles, New York, San Francisco and other cities. Flush with business, Meek expanded his finishing plant, making it the largest in the world.

The marble was first hauled down a steep, four-mile grade from the quarry to the finishing plant by teams of horses, then by a steam tractor and finally by an electric tram. On August 12, 1912, Meek and four others were bringing marble down from the quarry when the brakes failed on the tram and it ran out of con-

trol. Meek ordered the men to jump and did so himself but suffered fatal injuries in the fall. He died two days later. The jumps were unnecessary, however, since the marble blocks toppled from the speeding tram cars and, without their weight, the tram eventually stopped.

The marble operation languished after Meek's death but new management secured a contract for the Lincoln Memorial in Washington, D. C. The Memorial Commission wanted the whitest, soundest, most beautiful marble, regardless of cost. Work on the contract continued from 1914 to 1916 and called for cutting 36 columns 46 feet high and seven feet in diameter. Over 600 freight cars were needed to transport the marble, with each car carrying 50,000 to 70,000 pounds of stone.

Colorado-Yule Marble failed after World War I and was acquired by the

Vermont Marble Company of Proctor, Vermont, which won the contract for the Tomb of the Unknown Soldier in 1931. The tomb required the largest single block of marble ever quarried and 75 men took more than a year to cut the 105-ton block.

At the quarry, the block was trimmed down to 14x7.4x6 feet, and weighed 56 tons. A huge derrick was sent from Vermont to lift the block out of the quarry, and two electric trams - one in front, the other behind - were chained together to slowly skid the block down the tram grade to the mill. The four-mile trip took three days.

Armed guards at the mill prevented souvenir hunters from chipping at the massive block, which was put on a rail car, crated and braced, then shipped to Vermont. There it was trued to perfection with surveyor's instruments and shipped to Arlington Cemetery, where it was carved.

Despite the success of this challenge and the lasting quality of the marble, operations ceased in 1941 with the advent of World War II. Most of the mill machinery and equipment was disassembled and shipped out to key war industries under supervision of the War Production Board. The nearly deserted town of Marble never became a ghost town, but came close. Outdoor recreation kept the town alive with an Outward Bound School camp above town and road and trail access to the Elk Mountains.

During the 1970s developer Lee Stubblefield made an ambitious attempt to create a major ski area at Marble that would rival Aspen and Vail. A 4,200-foot chairlift was built on Mt. Daly, the base area for which was the million-dollar Marble Village Inn. The development soon ran into the burgeoning environmental ethic, where such growth was seen as a mortal foe to be defeated at any cost. A state geologist ruled the ski area was on unstable soil following a 1970's mud slide. While such slides are ever present in the Marble area, the ruling stalled development and the company floundered into bankruptcy. In the 1980s and again in the 1990s helicopter skiing was conducted in the area, but protests about flying over the Snowmass - Maroon Bells Wilderness and even Marble itself finally squelched those plans.

The vast stores of marble are of such a high quality that the quarry was reopened in 1989 under the historic name Colorado-Yule Marble Company. About 10,000 tons of marble are sold annually to Asia and Europe, where it's used for monuments. The quarried blocks are hauled down Highway 133 to Glenwood Springs by semi-trailer trucks, then shipped by rail to ports on either coast. At the rate of 10,000 tons a year the quarry could produce for several hundred more years.

The Death of David Davis

If working the marble quarry didn't carry enough risk for the men of Marble, the winter threat of avalanche certainly did. David Davis, the timekeeper at the Colorado-Yule quarry in 1912, had started for lunch at the boarding house. Head down, shoulders squared into a savage winter storm, Davis never saw the

The Colorado-Yule marble quarry was perched precariously on the face of the mountain of marble

The crane in the Yule quarry lifted the heavy blocks out of the quarry and down to the tram after they were cut.

avalanche that swept him from the road and carried him over a 120-foot drop. He was buried and smothered before he could utter a cry.

His brother, the Rev. H. Davis, a Presbyterian minister, came to retrieve the body, but the weather made his arriving in Marble impossible, as the storm continued to rage. The men of Marble were not about to allow a storm to deter them from removing the body for proper burial, however, and with great courage and greater determination they dug Davis from his snowy tomb.

According to a report in the Marble Booster of March 9, 1912, the entire town took notice a week after the fatal

avalanche when a grim procession started toward town.

"First there appeared about ten men in single file, and people in the town below could see how hard it was for them to get through the deep snow. Then there was a space of twenty-five yards and another line of thirty men, also in single file. The word spread through the town:

"'They are bringing down the body of David Davis.'

"The line of men were from the quarry. They had been shut in there by the storms for nearly a week with the dead body of their companion. Provisions were running short and they knew that it was urgent that the body

FRONTIER HISTORICAL SOCIETY MUSEUM OF GLENWOOD SPRINGS

The town of Prospect was located on the site of today's Darien Ranch at the base of Chair Mountain near the foot of McClure Pass. Genter and the Genter coal mine were later just west of Prospect. Schutte Collection Photo.

Tragedy on the Marble Tram

Bringing blocks of marble down from the quarry to the mill was an exciting and often deadly occupation for those with the skill and courage to operate the electric trolley. On one ill-fated trip, the brakes failed half a mile from the mill and the runaway trolley gained incredible speed. One passenger, a mill worker, jumped and escaped without a scratch. The other four weren't so lucky.

Just before the train reached the bridge over the Crystal River, near the mill, two of the cars left the track and smashed into a cliff. Robert Lytle, the brakeman, was thrown with great force into the face of the cliff and killed instantly. Lytle's son, Rush, who worked at the mill, witnessed his father's impact. He rushed to the body and held it while his father breathed his last.

On the final curve at the entrance to the yards, the rest of the train crashed and sent a tremor through the mill. A passenger, Atansio Negrete, was slammed to the ground and killed. Another passenger, eight-year-old Mary Tonko, was alive when rescuers found her but she died that evening. The motorman of the ill-fated trolley, George Healy, rode the speeding train until the end. The Marble Booster reported his demise.

"Witnesses said that Healy started from one side of the car to the other just as the final smash came. There was a huge block of marble just back of the trolley cab and Healy put up one hand to steady himself on this block just as the car turned over. The block caught him and fell squarely on top of him.

should be gotten to town. They decided to take chances on getting caught in slides along the way.

"The body of Davis was wrapped in canvas and securely lashed to a pair of skis, with a rope attached to pull it. The entire force of the quarry went ahead to break trail. It was a sight to be remembered-those men coming single file down the mountain."

"A young man employed at the mill by the name of McCann was only a few feet away when the smash came and he ran to the spot. He saw one of Healy's hands sticking out from beneath the block of marble and in the excitement of the moment he took hold of it. He said the hand grasped his firmly and then relaxed. He then saw the blood trickling out from under the rock and he knew it was all up for poor Healy."

Prospect

Tucked beneath Chair Mountain near the base of McClure Pass on the edge of a picture postcard meadow the town of Prospect was a coal mining camp owned by John Osgood and CF&I. It was also the site of Osgood's first ranch in the Crystal Valley, Prospect Ranch. The town was granted a Post Office in 1886 and its population peaked at 200. The railroad refueled at Prospect and when both coal and marble fortunes declined, so did the town.

A letter from mining engineer J. A. Kebler, one of Osgood's key lieutenants, to C.M. Schenck in 1886 describes conditions at Prospect as being rough and ready, with 70-80 men working several mines and guarding one claim with Winchesters. Kebler, who rode between the mines on horseback for weeks at a time, offers this (tongue-in-cheek) lexicon.

• Road: A space six feet wide, full of rocks, and with places as steep as the side of a house.

• Trail: A narrow path along almost inaccessible cliffs and with large logs across it, so steep in almost all places that you lead your horse uphill because he

POINTS OF INTEREST

Highway 133 from Carbondale to Paonia Reservoir, 47 miles.

• Begin at the Carbondale overlook on Highway 82, information and a scenic overview of Carbondale, farms and ranches and Mt. Sopris.

• Drive south on Highway 133, the West Elk Loop; Colorado Rocky Mountain School barn and campus on the west. Historical Society museum.

• Crystal Fish Hatchery, Crystal River, a view of the Eugene Grubb home tucked behind working ranch barns on the west.

• Turnouts for viewing Mt. Sopris.

• Mile marker 59 3/4 is a view of large white marble blocks, ballast along the railroad to keep the river from washing out the tracks.

• White River National Forest sign, mile marker 57 1/2, is across the river from the old Janeway stage stop on Avalanche flats. At mile marker 57 is the road to Avalanche Creek campground.

• Turnouts at either end of the granite narrows give views of dramatic scenery and a former quarry. Elk and big horn sheep graze along the river and an old railroad grade cuts through the rocky cliff. Penny Hot Springs (formerly Clinton) is on the riverbank.

• Redstone has two entrances, a mile apart; the north approach accesses the Redstone campground, the south one the village, museum, coke ovens and the coal miner memorial.

• A mile further is a turnout on the east with views of the Osgood mansion and estate. Hayes Creek Falls is at mile marker 49. Placita, a trailhead and an overlook are at mile marker 48.

• Turnoff to Marble, mile marker 46.

• McClure Pass, mile marker 43.

• Gateway to the Muddy country, Collbran, mile marker 33.

• Mudslide area, mile marker 27.5

• Paonia Reservoir, mile marker 25.

• Paonia Dam, mile marker 21.

cannot get up with you on and downhill from fear of falling over his head.

• Cabin: A rough log house about 10x12 with a dirt roof, the home of mountain rats, put on to collect the water when it rains so that the roof leaks for three days after every shower.

• Fireplace: A place on the floor of a cabin usually in the corner, with a hole in the roof to have the wind blow down and blow the smoke in your eyes. Almost all cabins have them but no one uses them.

• Mile: Measure of distance, usually about 18,000 feet. Distances here seem nothing; a man starts out on a 100-mile horseback trip as if he were driving downtown.

Paonia Reservoir to Crawford

In the early 1900s Somerset was the biggest coal mining town in the North Fork Valley, complete with company housing. The original discovery of Somerset coal was made by Ira Quimby Sanborn in 1883.

Somerset

From Paonia Dam near the north end of Kebler Pass, the North Fork canyon quickly becomes coal country. In less than three miles is the deserted mine camp of Oliver. Mines can be seen on either side of the Gunnison River and the town of Somerset, the first community, is just four miles farther.

In 1883 Ira Quimby Sanborn, a geologist, left the mining camp of Irwin, west of Crested Butte, crossed Kebler Pass and ventured into the North Fork of the Gunnison where he discovered rich deposits of anthracite coal. He began an enterprise that would later become a quaint community of cottages named for Somersetshire, England.

There was no railroad at the time, only rough wagon roads, but Sanborn opened a coal seam and began hand

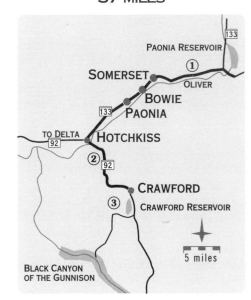

PAONIA RESERVOIR TO CRAWFORD
37 MILES

1. Oliver, West Elk coal mine and reclamation project, mile 18
2. The "Dobes," through mile 11 on Hwy 92
3. Black Canyon of the Gunnison access

mining coal, delivering it on horseback or by sled to blacksmiths in the North Fork valley. When Sanborn's wife died, leaving him with young children and little capital, his resolve weakened. The Panic of 1893 forced him to abandon his claims altogether.

Edd Hanson bought out Sanborn and sold the promising coal mine to the Utah Fuel Company in 1901, which then sold it to the Denver & Rio Grande Railroad in 1903. Colorado Fuel and Iron (CF&I) of Pueblo, the region's major steel manufacturer, was contracted to handle the mining of Sanborn's coal vein for the Rio Grande and used Somerset as a supply camp. Eighty tents housed miners and their families in a "tent city".

Once the Rio Grande pushed a narrow gauge up the North Fork and reached Somerset in 1903, the town's' prospects grew. In 1904 there were 12 carpenters hired to build permanent housing for the miners who worked four days a week to produce 75 cars of coal. Miners were paid $6.30 for ten-hour shifts and the Somerset mine became the largest underground mine in Colorado.

Somerset miners were Italian, Austrian, Welsh, Scottish, Finnish and Mexican. Many had been employed in European mines and they came to the U.S. for opportunity. By 1910 there were 135 miners at Somerset and 85 company-owned cottages, with a boarding house for single men. In 1911 Somerset was believed to be the only US Post Office without a wagon road to the outside, just rail.

The payroll came by train - in cash - and every miner was expected to be on hand to pick up his pay or it was returned

The Somerset Brass Band was comprised of local citizens with musical aptitudes. The band performed at special holidays and community events.

to the safe and shipped back to Utah until the following pay day. Marshal Tige Reed was company guard. He was called "Two Finger Tige", for a handicap that was not known to hamper his shooting. He met the train each night, and if anybody got off without a valid reason for being there, Tige locked him up for the night and sent him out on the next train.

By 1915, the mine had grown to 206 miners. Peak production occurred during World War I, when the mine employed 300 miners to meet wartime demands. Attesting to the size of the vein (14 feet thick), a single block of coal was removed in 1916 weighing 1,490 pounds. In the 1920s a starting miner was paid as low as $3.41 a day, or "kid's wages" as they were called. There was no instruction, so a novice had to learn quickly from an experienced partner.

Two mine fires, in 1911 and 1972, idled miners but were extinguished by flooding the burning levels. Economics proved more daunting than fire, however, and the single economy town wavered during hard times when coal production declined because of competition with natural gas and oil as heating fuels, and in light of railroads converting to diesel.

Between the 1950s and 1970s coal production suffered a severe nation-wide slump. Thousands of mines closed in the country, including several in the North Fork Valley. Somerset persevered until 1985 when, following 20 years of operation by US Steel, the mine closed, putting hundreds out of work and forcing many miners and their families to relocate and seek new professions.

The mine was purchased in 1990 by Pacific Basin Resources, a trading compa-

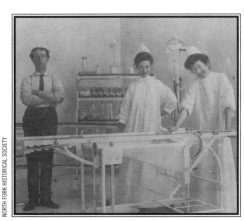

NORTH FORK HISTORICAL SOCIETY

Somerset even had a doctor's office.

ny which reopened the mine as Sanborn Creek Mine in 1991. Bear Coal Company was a minority partner. In 1995, Oxbow Carbon and Minerals purchased Bear's interest. The mine is currently operated exclusively by Oxbow, and as of early 1997 employed 137 workers.

Somerset was a classic company town on a par with stereotypical Appalachian communities built for one purpose - the mining of coal. In that tradition, Somerset's history describes a blue collar lifestyle and hard working ethic. Simple pleasures and a constant struggle for better working conditions were the chief interests of Somerset miners.

In the old days, good drinking water was scarce, so residents gathered at the railroad station and filled buckets from the water tanks on the train - leaving just enough for its return trip. Entertainment at the end of the line consisted of home-spun community dances, or "kitchen sweats", held in miner's cottages. Fiddles and accordions made merry tunes for the miners who danced their cares away.

Every worthwhile community of the day had a band and Somerset was no exception. Baseball was popular with miners and management alike - great pride was taken in the prowess of teams. It was said that a good ball player never had to worry about finding employment in Somerset.

Labor organizing has long been a source of controversy in mining towns, and Somerset was a flashpoint for the North Fork. During early organizing days, labor activists were not let off the train in the company town but were returned forcibly to Delta. Finally, in 1930, miners suffering under poor working conditions petitioned to join the United Mine Workers Union. In 1933 a union delegation came to hold meetings. The delegation was forbidden from meeting in Somerset and met instead across the river on private land. Later that year at a meeting in the Bowie dancehall near Paonia the miners took a mass oath and Somerset became a union town.

"God bless all the coal miners that took part in making our union very respectable, those who suffered through the old and stayed with the union," expressed one miner who valued his union benefits and the struggles of his union brothers.

The miner's cottages in Somerset, which had no indoor plumbing until the 1940s, were transferred to private ownership in the 1950s. The uniform gray buildings were transformed with fresh paint into individual homes, ending the stigma of the company town. Today, Somerset is primarily a retirement and coal worker's community. The town celebrated its centennial in September 1997.

MOUNTAIN COAL COMPANY

A long-wall mining machine at the West Elk Mine churns coal from a seam in the North Fork Valley. Hydraulic jacks support the roof of the cavern as the coal is undermined and carried away by conveyor.

Coal Mines of the North Fork

Enormous coal conveyors and tipples and long strings of coal cars on the Union Pacific rail line hauling 10,000 tons of coal a day are a testament to a long history of coal mining in the North Fork Valley. A massive vein of high quality coal - one of the largest in the world - lies between Glenwood Springs and Somerset, cropping up in Crested Butte and Floresta on the east and all the way northwest to the Colorado River under Grand Mesa!

When the Denver & Rio Grande announced plans to build a railroad to this coal bearing region in the late 1880s, many claims were filed under an 1873 act of Congress disposing of coal lands by priority of possession and improvement. An enterprising individual could claim 160 acres for $10 per acre if the claim was more than 15 miles from a railroad. The price went up to $20 per acre if it was

Mine workers construct a wall at the portal of a North Fork coal mine.

Coal wagons and horse teams were used to transport coal from the portal of the Black Diamond Mine. Conine's teams are pictured here in 1909.

nearer. An association could claim 320 acres under the act.

With the railroad pressing into the North Fork, it was prudent to make a claim before the Rio Grande arrived, and many did. Champion Coal, Hawk's Nest mines 1 and 2, Bear Coal Company, Oliver Coal Mine, Gilwick Mine and Black Beauty are among the names that made the North Fork a major coal concern.

The first big structure west of Somerset is a massive conveyor and silo system for one of the largest underground mines in the world, operated by the Atlantic Richfield Company. By using modern equipment and technology - the computerized long-wall technique - this mine has set world records in production and ships as much as 6 million tons in a year. The Atlantic Richfield mine is located where the Bear Mine opened in 1935, across the river from the former Bowie Mine, which opened in the early 1900s.

A quarter mile west of the old power plant a new road to the north leads to a new mine opened by Bowie Resources which purchased the property from Coors Energy Company. The mine plans to produce in excess of 1 million tons of coal a year.

Further west, at the intersection of Highway 133 and the turn-off to Paonia, a road leading north goes to a mine that was opened by the Colorado Westmoreland Company in 1976. The mine prospered until a devastating mine fire in 1986. Paonia residents could see smoke and flames shooting from the portals. The fire, started by spontaneous combustion, was extinguished by plugging the portals with hundreds of tons of sand and starving the fire of oxygen. The mine reopened from another portal in January 1987.

Many mines of the North Fork began as family operations or "wagon mines", sometimes run by just mom and pop. Or, as was the case with the Emmons family, nine brothers worked the seam. Many local coal customers were cash poor so they traded goods and services - flour, beef and produce - as barter with coal producers.

The Farmer's Mine was a cooperative venture among a group of farmers who purchased shares of the mine for $50, thus earning the privilege of mining the coal themselves for domestic use. Later, the mine went commercial and each

The Conine Mine has changed since this 1909 photograph. It became the Cowan Mine later that year, then was incorporated as Farmer's Progressive Coal Company in 1912. Since 1981 the mine has been owned and operated by the Westmoreland Coal Company as the Orchard Mine.

investor received a share of the profits.

Coal mining in the North Fork has always been a story of hard work by those who went underground with pick and shovel, and who often went days without seeing sunlight. These values are told by the story of the Hawk's Nest Mine, which was opened by Clement Audin, a young man from Belgium. He began mining in his home country in the 1880s at age 11, hand picking coal for 18 cents a day.

After he moved to the North Fork in the 1920s Audin went to work at a local mine where he mined coal 14 hours a day, six days a week. With his earnings the enterprising miner gradually realized the personal dream of owning a small dairy herd. After a long day at the mine, which started at 4 a.m., Audin returned home to pitch hay to his dairy stock at night, by lantern light.

During the winter Audin mended shoes for fellow miners. After scrupulously saving his money Audin purchased a mining claim of his own. In 1932 he began work-ing his Hawk's Nest Mine with sons Ralph, Abel and Clem Jr. Together, they made the mine one of the richest in the North Fork.

Not everyone found success for their labors, however. A story tells of a young, itinerant miner who worked two winters for the owner of the Gilwick Mine. Toward the end of the young man's stay it became apparent that the owner was cash poor and could not afford to pay him for his labor with anything but an old, white mule. The young man pondered the offer, grudgingly took the mule, and left the valley.

Coal mines have long been the bread and butter for many a North Fork family who were marked indelibly by the mining lifestyle. The unforgettable ambiance of the mines created a powerful personal memory as described by Billy Spohr Ungaro of Paonia. When Ungaro was a boy, his father took him on a mine tour where he smelled the blended fragrance of acrid carbide lanterns and pungent Jacks and Jennies, the working mules. "The peculiar odor, and the blackness of the darkness, is a memory that has never left me," said Ungaro.

Bowie

Bowie speaks of the tenuous nature of western settlement and industrial development. The boom and bust cycle brought prosperity and then fail-ure to many of these once-prominent coal mines.

Bowie sprang up in the early 1900s sev-eral miles east of Paonia. Just north of the old power plant, on the north side of the valley, are the remains of a tramway that came from the mine portal. The

The upper works of the Bowie Mine in 1910.

town and the mine were first named "Juanita" for the daughter of mine superintendent, Henry Mallot. The town would later be named Bowie for Alexander Bowie, who became the general manager of the Juanita in 1906 after having emigrated from Scotland with his father in 1866.

Coal mining was in Alexander Bowie's blood from the beginning. He began working at the collieries in Scotland at age 10. Still young when he reached the US, Bowie went to the coal fields of Ohio, Pennsylvania and West Virginia as a seasoned veteran. Bowie studied mine engineering and earned his Inspector Certificate. In 1877 he was named the first Mine Inspector of the State of Pennsylvania. Bowie soon married and the family moved to New Mexico, where Bowie became general manager for the Caledonia Coal Company, and later its president. In 1906 he sold his interest in Caledonia and invested in the Juanita Mine.

Bowie moved to Colorado to assume his new post and he became the first postmaster of Juanita, which later took the name Bowie by decree of the Postal Service; Juanita was apparently too similar to another established post office. The mine already had a boarding house, bunk house, stable, blacksmith shop and steam plant, which were erected in 1903. The Denver & Rio Grande Railroad broadguaged its tracks through the North Fork in 1906. A year later a tramway was built to the tipple.

Coal was blasted loose with black powder charges and the mine was ventilated by steam - powered fans. Tenant houses were built by 1915 and Bowie took on the character of a full-fledged town. The Bowie family residence, a stately brick home for the general manager, was built in 1914. In 1922 a brick power plant housed two 375-kilowatt turbine-driven generators. In 1920 the mine reached peak production with 110 miners producing 103,622 tons that year. By 1956, thanks to technological advances in mining, all the mine mules but one were retired. The last mule was kept on for odd jobs.

In a mining accident, Alexander Bowie lost a leg in 1935, but that didn't seem to slow him from his goal of making the Juanita a large producer and Bowie a model mining town. The Bowies had 11 children, many of whom took part in mining operations as their aging but active father turned over management duties.

The vagaries of the coal economy eventually conspired to shut down the Bowie mine. The entire operation - town and all - was sold to the Adolph Coors Company in 1974. Some of the tenant homes were moved and others demolished for salvage. Coors donated much of the Bowie mining machinery to the State Historical Society, which displays it in Denver.

The general manager's house was relocated to Midway in the 1990s, the old midway point between Paonia and Hotchkiss,

THE BOWIE BOAT

The unique feature of Bowie was an innovation used by coal miners when the whistle blew at the end of their shifts. The "boat" became the vehicle of choice for descending the steep railroad track from the mine portal. Devised by an ingenious miner, Eugene Fronk in 1908, the boat was a grooved piece of wood that fit over the rail. The miners sat on the boat, tucked their legs beneath them, clasped their lunch pails between their legs, and slid down the rail. They used one arm as an outrigger to the other rail, while the other arm controlled a brake fashioned from rubber hose. By plying the brake against the rail, the boat allowed them to cruise downhill at a steady and exciting 15 miles per hour.

The boat was not without risk. In rain or snow the tracks would become slippery, rendering the brake ineffective. When a new miner finally warmed up to the idea, he found great pleasure in leaving his shift, not only because it was the end of the work day, but for a rip-roaring ride down the tracks.

Construction of the Fire Mountain Canal, one of many vital conduits to fruit orchards of the North Fork.

where it serves as a private home. The Bowie schoolhouse was moved to Paonia where it serves as an exhibit at the Paonia Historical Society museum.

Oliver

The Oliver Mine was about five miles upstream from Bowie. It was opened in 1924 by Charles Oliver with a 23-man mining operation.

Through the 1920s, "Red Glow Coal" from the Oliver was hauled by truck to Somerset and loaded into rail cars. In 1927 the Oliver produced over 1,000 cars of high quality coal. Enticed by strong production and a good market, the Rio Grande built a spur to Oliver - the "Oliver Short Line"- in 1928. In 1930, the Oliver Power Plant electrified the mine with a coal-burning generator that was later purchased by Western Power Company.

In 1943 an entrance was opened across the river and a railroad spur hauled coal to the tipple. The Oliver was since closed.

A burro built for two.

Pioneers Lee Young and family at their homestead cabin in 1906.

Paonia

Like a nest in a royal garden,
Where the birds are soothed with song
Through the day, aflame with glory,
And cradled the fair night long;
Like a rose in a sheltered arbor,
Smiling the livelong day
Lies the beautiful town - Paonia -
Where the North Fork wends its way.

- from "Paonia"
by Dr. E. F. Eldridge, 1905

Named for the Peony flower, in its Latin spelling - Paeonia - by its founder, Samuel Wade, Paonia is a story of bold pioneering, undaunted vision and economic diversity, all wrapped in a gentle climate, a rich river valley, and an array of fertile mesas watered by the creeks and streams of the West Elk Mountains and Grand Mesa.

Samuel Wade first came to the North Fork Valley in 1881 with the Duke brothers and Enos Hotchkiss, founder of the town bearing his name ten miles down river. The settlers advanced as the Ute Indians retreated, pushed out of Western Colorado and onto a Utah reservation by U.S. troops in September 1881.

Wade was no stranger to Indians. He became a close friend to Ute Chief Ouray and was known as an Indian fighter for his role in the war against the Sioux in the Black Hills of South Dakota. His son Ezra describes his father in the aftermath of the bloody battle of Whitestone Hill. "Father said he walked out over the battleground alone among the wounded. He came upon an old Indian woman who had been shot, lying with her head downhill. Seeing she was alive, he picked her up by the arms and placed her in a more comfortable position. As he did so she looked up and smiled."

Wade noticed several Indian babies lying near their dead mothers. "They were sound asleep. After returning to camp, a Private soldier asked him to go over the battleground with him. Father went. When they came to an Indian baby, the Private pulled out his revolver and shot the baby in the head. Father was very angry and thought of proffering charges against the Private, but after reconsidering their own losses, which were not small, and the awful tragedies caused to the Whites by the Sioux Indians, he dropped the case."

Paonia fruit orchards brought the community prominence in the 1880s and continue fueling a healthy agricultural economy today. The wind tower is powered by an airplane engine that stirs the air in case of a frost, protecting young fruit.

Ditch building required a crew of dedicated and interested parties sharing mutual labor for mutual benefits. The Fire Mountain canal was a big job.

After achieving the rank of Captain when he was mustered out of the U.S. Army at the end of the Civil War, Samuel Wade took his family to Butler, Missouri where he employed his civil engineering background as an architect and builder. Among his accomplishments was surveying the town of Pleasanton, Kansas. Driven from the Midwest by drought in 1874, Wade herded his livestock to Colorado with his sons Ezra, 14, and George, 19. Ezra describes their journey.

"A big storm set in and it snowed hard, then turned bitterly cold. When night came we went into camp. We had no wood. What were we to do? It looked as though we would perish. We were camped near the railroad. The first train that passed us threw off some coal, for which we were thankful."

When they reached the San Luis Valley in south central Colorado, having fought bitter cold through the mountains, the Wades came to the end of the wagon road. Headed further west to the settlement of Saguache, the cattle and horses had to go without water for 56 hours. The family finally reached Saguache, the doorstep to the Gunnison Country, on January 1, 1875.

Samuel Wade's ultimate destination was further west still in the booming mining district of Lake City, 300 miles from the nearest railroad and a gold miner's utopia on the edge of the rich San Juan Mountains. "The country was alive with excitement,"

effused Ezra."Every fellow had a bonanza! Carpenters worked day and night."

After a stint in Lake City, Wade settled in Pitkin, a community east of Gunnison where he operated a sawmill. Samuel made new plans when friends journeyed to the unknown North Fork Valley and returned with a glowing report. "They came upon a little valley in a part of the state that had a fine climate and was good country, but the Indians would not let them stop there long."

Wade sold his sawmill in Pitkin and returned to Lake City, where he and Enos Hotchkiss decided to explore the "new country" for themselves in August 1881, just one month before the Utes were moved to Utah. "Upon their return," reported Ezra, "Father and Enos were the most enthusiastic men I have ever seen. Father said it was fruit country, one where we could raise peaches and apricots."

A month later, the men returned to the North Fork with the intention of estab-

The fruit of the bounteous North Fork Valley was immortalized by the photographer W. S. Edwards, who portrayed in stylized glass plate photographs an incomparable history of the valley. These photos are from 1908.

W. S. Edwards, photographer

lishing a permanent settlement in the rich, pastoral valley. As the Utes reluctantly retreated west, Samuel Wade, Enos Hotchkiss and the Duke brothers followed Indian trails to the best fords in the North Fork River. One river ford was at the present site of Paonia, and Wade chose it as his farm.

"On the first of September, 1881, E. T. Hotchkiss, myself and others came into the Valley of the North Fork," wrote Samuel Wade in 1885, "and while making a stay of only one day, I discovered thorn apple and buffalo berry growing luxuriantly and in abundance. Therefore, with this evidence before me, I became strongly of the belief that many varieties of fruit might be grown here and resolved at once to make the trial."

The valley was prime growing ground, wrote Ezra Wade when he viewed the site selected by his father. "The river was very crooked, which lessened its fall; therefore, it did not cut its banks, but spread over a large portion of the valley during high-water, depositing sand and rich soil from the high country, making the valley soil, in places, very rich. There were many deer and brown bear, and lots of elk...Our camp was well supplied with venison. Anyone could kill a deer those days. They were not very wild and easy to find. They would almost come up to you, but with bear it was different. Those old fellows would fight. The North Fork River had a lot of trout. There were lots of beaver along the river."

To prove his theory about fruit growing, Wade picked up a shipment of fruit trees the next April, 1882, at the railhead at Sapinero, near the Blue Mesa dam at present day US Highway 50. He loaded them into a wagon equipped with sled runners for a spring crossing on snow. His shipment consisted of 200 apple trees of different varieties, 10 pears, 10 apricots, 20 peaches, 200 cherries, five quinces, 100 grape vines, 1,000 blackberries, 100 raspberries, 12 currants, 50 gooseberries, 500 maples and various ornamentals.

The Wades, Ernest Yoakum and his two sons drove the wagon over rugged and roadless Black Mesa, sledding across the frozen snow in the early mornings until the spring sun softened it too much for travel. They burned fires at night to keep the fruit trees from freezing. "After shoveling snow for about three weeks on the Black Mesa," recalled Samuel Wade, "I succeeded in getting onto my ranch, on the 21st day of April, 1882 ...I proceeded to clear up the ground and to build a two-mile ditch for the purpose of irrigating these trees and

Cady's Pipeline in 1909, constructed by a private water company, was made of wood banded by iron hoops. This was common for early city water lines.

WILLIAM BEAR SR.

Smoke from the Colorado Westmoreland Orchard Mine fire darkened the skies over Paonia on June 2, 1986.

such crop of grain and vegetable as I might be able to get in that spring."

In his initial planting, Wade lost one-third of his fruit trees, but after replanting he proved his claim that the North Fork was prime for orchards. Next, Wade freighted in a small stock of merchandise and established a store in one room of his log house. Merchandise was shipped by wagon over steep Black Mesa, where logs were tied to the wagons to slow their speed on the downhill run.

A post office was established in Paonia during the summer of 1882, Wade being appointed post master. The office was located in his store.

In 1883 the Paonia School District was organized and built the first school. Jesse Yoakum was hired as the first teacher for $30 a month. Classes met in a log building with mud roof and potbellied stove. A brick schoolhouse replaced the 16 x 24 log structure in 1895. Paonia High School was built in 1904, and the first class - three girls - graduated that year. The first boy graduated in 1907.

An elaborate system of irrigation ditches was needed, and the Wade and Clarke Ditch, which tapped Minnesota Creek, was the first. By 1900, a dozen ditches were completed or under construction to irrigate the thriving fruit industry. Wagon loads of fruit rumbled down the dusty road toward Delta and nearby mining towns.

W. S. Coburn and Samuel Wade took six first places with fruit they exhibited at the 1893 World's Fair in Chicago, and once the Denver & Rio Grande railroad pushed its line into the North Fork from Delta in 1902 - the year of Paonia's incorporation - the region boomed with record fruit production.

Early transportation in Paonia included this dapper gentleman and his Indian motorcycle, loaded for touring.

Captain Jack Sinclair's Cowboy Band on the main street of downtown Paonia.

By 1904 two firms handled Paonia fruit - the North Fork Fruit Growers Association and Nelson Brothers, shipping hundreds of railroad cars full of fruit. The same year, according to the "*Paonia Booster*", the prospering town had a schoolhouse, three churches, two banks, 22 mercantile establishments, two weekly newspapers and an electric light plant.

"The business growth of Paonia has kept step with the increase in population," proclaimed the *Souvenir*, a promotional book published in 1905. "Paonia has become a city of thrift and intelligence. Her schools are second to none, her churches are numerous... Paonia boasts as neat and clean stocks of merchandise as can be found on the entire Western Slope."

The peak of the fruit industry occurred in the early 1900s when fruit orchards spread from Paonia to Hotchkiss, up Minnesota Creek and across the sunny mesas rising above the valley floor. Later falling fruit

prices, killer frosts and insect infestations conspired to dishearten growers who suffered failure and financial ruin.

Fruit was not the only economic engine to speed Paonia on its way. Cattle ranching and coal mining formed the other two legs of the tripod on which Paonia found economic stability that has made it a lasting community.

The first cattle came to the region in the late 1880s and grazed in the foothills of the Elk Mountains during summer and among the "dobes", or adobe hills between Paonia and Crawford, during the winter. Before the railroad came to the North Fork in 1902 cattle were pushed from summer range near Terror Creek, the Muddy country and Minnesota Creek over McClure pass to the Placita railhead near Redstone. By the early 1890s, sheep began to appear on the range.

Mining became an economic mainstay of the Paonia area that gained considerable prominence in the already successful fruit growing region once settlers appreciated its usefulness. The first settlers, unaware of the value of coal, burned cottonwood logs from the river bottom as their main source of heat. Charcoal for blacksmith shops was made from willows.

Despite fluctuations in the fruit industry, in 1947 the town initiated Cherry Day, a lasting tradition that honors the fruit economy every July 4. This parade and town park celebration brings Paonians together for reunions. In the early days, free bags of cherries were given to all in attendance. A Cherry Day Queen is chosen each year.

After serving a term in the State Legislature in 1887, Paonia's founder,

The miner's memorial statue in Paonia honors all the coal miners killed in North Fork coal mine accidents.

"Togo" was a well-known trotting horse in Paonia in 1911.

Samuel Wade, sold his orchard and ranch. He left his beloved North Fork Valley for Blaine, Washington. He died in 1904 and is buried in the Paonia cemetery.

Today, Wade's vision accounts for a lucrative agricultural enterprise that has evolved into an idealized agrarian lifestyle for many who have found in Paonia, as he did, a veritable cornucopia. Fruit and vegetable growing, coal mining and tourism are the major economic forces in the region, and an emerging wine grape industry holds future promise.

A song of praise for Paonia written in 1915 by Nellie Lange Skrydstrup celebrates the town's pride and perseverance:

There's an ideal little city
Surrounded by mountains grand
On the Western Slope of Colorado lands.
It is beautiful Paonia, the pride of all
  the West
Of which all nature has with splendor
  blessed.

Paonia's Pious Populous

Sometime in the 1930s, the popular Ripley's *Believe It or Not* featured Paonia as having the most churches per capita of any town or city in the U.S. In 1965 an article in the Denver Post corroborated Ripley by reporting 16 churches for a population of 1,080 - a church for every 67 residents. In the most recent accounting, Paonia has 13 churches - after mergers of congregations - for a population of 1,500. That's still respectable, proving Paonia's populous is indeed pious.

The North Fork Historical Society

On July 4, 1974, the North Fork Historical and Preservation Society was established to protect and interpret historical resources of the Paonia and North Fork area. The Society's existence can be credited to the efforts of a key individual - Wallace Eubanks.

Eubanks, an historian whose maternal roots are in Paonia, spent years gathering items of significance to the area history. They are incorporated in an interpretive museum and authentic school house near the banks of the North Fork of the Gunnison River at the Highway 133 entrance to Paonia.

Enos T. Hotchkiss, founder of Paonia.

The Duke family homestead in Hotchkiss, 1883.

In 1995, Ken Parks, a Paonia native, gave the museum house to the Society. This house was built in 1904 in the small community of Midway - halfway between Paonia and Hotchkiss - by his father, James Parks, who came to Paonia in a covered wagon. The house was used for boarding school teachers until James Park's wife, Cora, took up residence there in her later years. The house had no indoor plumbing because Cora preferred it that way.

The Parks house depicts the interior of a turn-of-the-century farmhouse and displays historic artifacts. Next door to the house is the Bowie School House, built in the early 1900s. After the town of Bowie was purchased by the Adolph Coors Company in 1974, the school was moved to its present location.

Museum hours - summer only - are Tuesday, Thursday and Saturday, 1-4 p.m. The museum is otherwise open by appointment. Contact Judy Livingston, Society president, (970) 527-3970.

Hotchkiss

Enos T. Hotchkiss is the father of two western Colorado towns - the one that bears his name in the North Fork Valley and the once booming mining town of Lake City, located on the Lake Fork of the Gunnison River at the edge of the San Juan Mountains. Both towns are on tributaries to the Gunnison River, separated by many miles of rugged mountain country that Hotchkiss knew well.

Born in 1835 in Bradford, Pennsylvania, Hotchkiss came west when he was 23. On horseback he traveled the wild Western Slope, evading Ute Indians as he followed the North Fork of the Gunnison in 1879. He recognized the promise of the region but was told by the Utes to leave.

Two years later he teamed up with the Duke brothers who had been hired to transport horses for him from Pueblo. Hotchkiss had been able to dissuade the Dukes from searching for gold with the legions of prospectors heading for the San

Juans and instead convinced them to accompany him to the "new country" in the North Fork.

After learning of the Ute's imminent departure, Hotchkiss, the Dukes and Samuel Wade entered the North Fork Valley. While Ute campfires still smoldered, the men hid in the dense sagebrush that crowded around ancient cottonwoods spreading along the meanders of the North Fork River and staked out their ranches. Hotchkiss chose the present townsite of Hotchkiss as his ranch.

The men had journeyed from the Gunnison Country over Black Mesa with two wagons, one pulled by a team of eight horses, the other by eight oxen. Theirs were the first wagons to enter the North Fork Valley, let alone cross the heavily timbered and roadless Black Mesa.

George Duke was the first to make his claim and the first to build his cabin. The First State Bank of Hotchkiss is located on

Horse packers prepare for a trip from downtown Hotchkiss, in front of the Hotchkiss Opera House, in the late 1800s.

HOTCHKISS HISTORICAL MUSEUM

Clara Duke, Will Duke, and Slattery Duke.

the southwest corner of George Duke's original hay field.

In 1882, the fledgling town was named Hotchkiss by George Duke, who was its first mayor. A post office was located in the home of Enos Hotchkiss where George Duke served as postmaster. A school teacher, Etta Gould, was hired and held classes that year. In 1883 the first fruit was planted and quickly became the economic mainstay. By 1886 a horticultural exhibit was held in Hotchkiss to promote the new fruit capital, and in 1904 1,000 train cars filled with fruit were shipped from the North Fork Valley, 50 percent of which came from Hotchkiss orchards.

While Enos Hotchkiss was honored by the town's name, he took a back seat in its development, allowing the Duke brothers to become the major influence. "Mr. Hotchkiss had not political aspira-

tions," reported the *Souvenir* in a 1905 tribute to the pioneer, "although the community continually importuned him to accept numerous positions of trust which he declined with the exception of one term of County Commissioner." Instead, it was the Duke brothers who invested themselves heart and soul in the town of Hotchkiss.

Originally from Onarga, Illinois, George Duke was a wheelwright who built the first cabin in the North Fork, was the first postmaster, the first assessor and the first mayor. He and his brothers established a lucrative mercantile trade with a department store that grossed $70,000 a year by the turn of the century.

"Identified with the North Fork, developing their resources with the growth of the country, and connected with the largest enterprises and business interests

of the section is the firm of Duke Brothers Co.," read an early promotion. The Duke brothers were quick to diversify into cattle, which they grazed in the Muddy country. In 1893 they established The Bank of the North Fork and were instrumental in funding the Fruit Exchange Bank in Paonia. In 1899, the Dukes and other partners dug the 21-mile Overland Ditch to irrigate Paine's Mesa, later known as Redlands Mesa.

The Dukes bought 500 acres to plant with apples, peaches and pears in 1900 and were said to own most of the valuable land on all the mesas north and south of the North Fork of the Gunnison. They "controlled" the North Fork Valley and were considered the wealthiest men in the region.

In 1905 the *Souvenir* reported the success of the town of Hotchkiss. "One hundred and nineteen cars of cattle were shipped last year. More than sixty thousand dollars worth of fruit was shipped during the same period. At least five hundred thousand dollars is invested in the

A blacksmith shop in Hotchkiss owned by Thomas Jackson "TJ" Smith, includes TJ and son Clyde "Young Jack" in 1909.

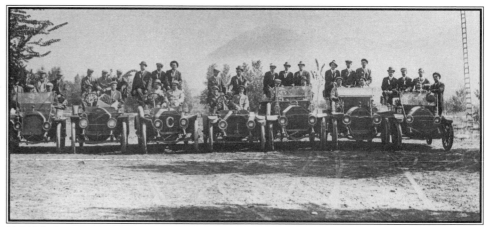

Model T Fords line up in Hotchkiss during a celebration at the fairgrounds.

A high diver at the Hotchkiss Fairgrounds.

banking business. Over one hundred thousand dollars has been expended in the improvement of the town itself with the best of prospects of over fifty thousand dollars being expended during the coming year. It is a natural business

nucleus of all the surrounding towns within a radius of ten miles in all directions and bids fair to be one of the leading business centers of the Western Slope."

Not enough good could be said about the North Fork's idyllic weather and excellent growing conditions, and Hotchkiss was the gem in the valley's crown. "It is the happy medium in altitude that brings beneficial results to the invalid," proclaimed the *Souvenir*.

"Protection by the surrounding high mountains and ranges from the severe winds of the plains and from the heavy snows of the north bring about this condition. No cyclone, forest fires, floods or other disturbances so prevalent in other sections of the country disturb the peaceful residents of this valley... The fruit crop is so prolific that it is necessary often times for the fruit grower to knock or pick off sometimes 50 percent of their burden, for if this were not done the trees would break with their load of fruit."

Like its neighbor Paonia, Hotchkiss

enjoyed a diverse economy that included cattle and mining. The Rio Grande provided rail transport by 1902, and the community seemed destined for greatness. The Hotchkiss Fruit Company promoted and marketed Hotchkiss fruit as far away as New York City and Chicago, a large general store sold agricultural implements, a drug store opened in 1901 and a candy store offered confections, ice cream and oysters.

The Fruitland Realty and Investment Company offered fire and life insurance and loaned money "at the lowest current rate." The North Fork Times became the newspaper of record, featuring columns, news items and editorials by editor Luther W. Rood, as a promotion described. "The majority of western towns are deficient in the newspaper line. Not so, however, for the metropolis, Hotchkiss, which is fortunately blessed with a newspaper editor who is willing to tell the truth at any and all times."

The Hotchkiss Hotel, which celebrated

Fruit pickers pause for a portrait in a Hotchkiss peach orchard.

A woman carefully wraps pears for shipping from a Hotchkiss packing shed.

its centennial in September 1997, stood out in Hotchkiss as a two-story brick structure that could accommodate 50 guests. "The building is fitted with baths, hot and cold water, bus runs to and from all trains and a first-class livery is in connection. The Hotchkiss hotel is rapidly becoming noted as one of the best places to stop on the Western Slope."

Today, Hotchkiss is a quiet, rural, retirement community of about 900 residents. Agriculture is still the economic base. The Fairgrounds is the site of the Delta County Fair on the first full week of August. A mid-summer festival is also held, as is the Black Canyon Arts Festival and the Colorado Grand, a 1000 - mile sports cars rally that stops in Hotchkiss.

Gold Medal Orchards

The produce of the North Fork Valley has been legendary since the first fruit crops in the 1890s. At the Chicago Columbian Exposition of 1893, the great world's fair that featured the first Ferris Wheel and Little Egypt, a belly dancer, fruit from the North Fork trees took gold medals in every category entered: six in all. Horticulturists proclaimed this high altitude fruit region a utopia.

Credit for the bounty was given to the virgin desert soil, which proved to be perfect for fruit growing, so perfect it produced prize winning fruit, copious yields and considerable profits for fruit growers. It was said that a fruit tree began producing here at the age of two years and in another year were producing a full crop.

There was the famed "Paonia Apple", an apparent mutant with a circumference of two feet and a nine-inch diameter. Vegetables also grew to inordinate proportions, especially potatoes, one of which attained the world's record of 11 pounds. As the soil grew weary, however, insects arrived and began to cripple the fruit trees. Still, Paonia sweet cherries retained a hallowed place as one of the best-flavored cherries in the world, and still do.

The Hotchkiss Historical Museum

The Hotchkiss Historical Society was formed in 1974 and offered displays of the town's history with borrowed photographs and donated artifacts. The museum was first housed in the town library and featured a few showcases. It was later moved to the old Hotchkiss Hotel, then to the Town of Crawford.

When the Society was given its current space in the American Legion Hall, the museum relocated to Hotchkiss.

The Museum features a carousel of historic photographs, an extensive barbed wire display, a collection of Ute and other Indian artifacts, and period collections of clothing and equipment depicting ranching and home life from the pioneer era.

The Hotchkiss Museum is located on Second Street one block from Highway 133 in the American Legion Hall. Hours are 1 to 4 p.m. Fridays, or otherwise by appointment.

Crawford

Unlike its fruit-growing neighbors, Paonia and Hotchkiss, Crawford was founded on an economy of cattle, hay and grain. Too high for economically viable fruit growing and too far from coal deposits, Crawford was cattle country. It still is. It was first settled by cattlemen who grazed their herds on summer mountain pastures and wintered them on the "dobes," adobe hills that range in gentle undulations down toward the North Fork Valley.

Crawford was established on the Smith Fork of the Gunnison River in the early 1880s and was granted a post office in 1887. The town was named for Captain George Crawford, an early pioneer who, when passing through in 1882, remarked to town founder Harry Grant that the region needed a post office. Grant took the suggestion seriously and applied for a post office, naming the fledgling town for the visionary captain who had since gone on his way.

HOTCHKISS HISTORICAL MUSEUM

Brokaw's Saloon was one of the first watering holes in Hotchkiss. Part of the attraction, aside from locally brewed beer, was a pair of bear cubs held by brothers Melvin and Ellis Wilson.

BROKAW'S SALOON

Like all western towns, the saloon figured prominently in Hotchkiss. The chief server of libations was M. M. Brokaw, whose saloon was known as Brokaw's Place. Neef Brothers beer was a special offering, advertised as "The Beer that will make Colorado Famous!"

But the most outstanding feature in Brokaw's Place was a pair of bear cubs, "Johnny" and "Molly," which served as mascots after their mother was killed by hunters. "The finest brands of whiskey and cigars are always to be found at Brokaw's... The visiting tourist who seeks a resort of this character will not be disappointed."

NORTH FORK HISTORICAL SOCIETY

The original townsite of Crawford in 1900 was located on the south side of the Smith Fork and included the Smith home (right) and the Co-op Store (left). Across the Smith Fork, at the present site of Crawford, is Mrs. Ong's store.

In 1889, a small store offering provisions for early settlers was opened in Crawford. By 1905 the town contained two general mercantile stores, a drug store, doctor's office, blacksmith shop, hotel, barber shop, city hall, meat market, lumber mill and church. A two-story stone schoolhouse was built in 1906 for $16,000.

While Crawford trailed behind Paonia and Hotchkiss in time and scale, the Crawford country of the Smith Fork was visited first by white settlers. Samuel Wade, Enos Hotchkiss and the Duke brothers passed through the Crawford country in 1881 after making their way over Black Mesa on their way to founding those towns.

Larry Barnard, an early settler in the Needle Rock area, first came to the Smith Fork from the Sapinero railhead in the 1880s, hiking across Black Mesa with only a pound of cheese and a box of crackers. Nick Newberg, a homesteader on Grandview Mesa, walked to the Smith Fork from Oklahoma, liked what he saw, and walked back to bring his family west.

Crawford remains a ranching and agricultural community, quiet and rural and somewhat remote. Recreational amenities at Paonia and Crawford Reservoirs and the Black Canyon north rim contribute to the local tourist economy. In the summer of 1997, British blues singer Joe Cocker and his wife, Pam, gentrified a portion of the downtown and started a trend of catering to tourism. They rebuilt the original bank and mercantile building and it now houses their Mad Dog restaurant and ice cream parlor, a bakery, space for retail botiques and a community room By the spring of 1998, Crawford had a half dozen restaurants.

A number of historic structures warrant attention. The Crawford Community Church, which stands prominently at the downtown curve of Highway 92, was built in 1900. The Crawford schoolhouse, built from stone quarried from the Smith Fork canyon, burned in 1912. It was rebuilt to serve all 12 grades until 1962, after which students were bussed to Hotchkiss. Designated a state historical site in 1994 it serves as the town hall, library and community center. Other places of interest are the Crawford cemetery - the "Garden of Memories" - Crawford General Store, Crawford State Bank and the K. C. Collins house, a prominent stone house built in 1910.

The Reign of the Cattlemen

Sam Hartman, one of the more colorful characters of the Crawford country, became the undisputed cattle king of the region during the 1880s and '90s, and cut a dashing figure of a cowboy and cattle rancher. Hartman's family came to the plains of eastern Colorado with the earliest pioneers. As a youngster, Sam rode the prairies, rounding up strays for neighboring ranchers.

When Sam was 17, the Hartman family ventured west to the settlement of Saguache in the San Luis Valley where the wagon road ended. Sam continued on horseback over Cochetopa Pass, following the Ute Indian trail into the Gunnison country. He joined his brother, Alonzo, at the original Los Pinos Agency where he worked for the federal government distributing beef to the Utes.

Daniel Boone was said to be an ancestor of the Hartmans, so it's no wonder the two brothers followed the ragged fringe of the frontier into unknown lands. Sam Hartman followed his brother as the Indian Agency was relocated from

The Crawford Schoobouse, built in 1906, burned in 1912. It currently serves as a community center.

In the early 1900s, Alva Reeder's children had to cross the Smith Fork Canyon to get to school in Crawford. Alva built two ladders for the purpose, both 18 feet long, plus rock steps and a winding trail.

Samuel B. Hartman was the biggest cattleman in the Crawford country.

Cochetopa Pass to the Uncompahgre Valley near Montrose. On the way, he explored Soap and Curecanti Creeks near the Black Canyon and in 1880 crossed Black Mesa and entered the Smith Fork.

In the fall of 1881, Sam Hartman and his partner Ed Kreighton were in Sapinero when they met a wagon train driving a herd of shorthorn cattle. Winter was coming on and the wagon train had no feed for the livestock. Sam bought the herd cheap and, with Kreighton, drove it over Black Mesa to the Smith Fork where Hartman had already put up a crop of wild hay on which the cattle wintered. He drove the herd to Hotchkiss the following spring and sold it to new settlers for a profit.

Hartman and Kreighton raised cattle in the Crawford area for many years, providing settlers with milk and beef. Hartman was the first rancher to sow oats and reap a grain crop on the Smith Fork. By 1889 Hartman owned 640 acres and ran 1,000 head of cattle. He delivered beef on the hoof as far away as Glenwood Springs,

driving them along the old Ute Trail over McClure Pass. In 1891, Hartman and Kreighton together ran 4,500 cows and calves on Soap Mesa near Sapinero, where they could readily ship their cattle to market by the Rio Grande.

Hartman diversified his holdings with business investments and became a large stockholder in the First Exchange Bank of Paonia, the North Fork Bank of Hotchkiss, the First National Bank of Gunnison, and a number of other businesses. In the 1890s, Kreighton inherited some money, and rather than "just ranching here until it was all gone," sold Hartman his interest and moved to Cuba, where there were no worries about winter feed for cattle.

In 1904, at age 45, Hartman had a seri-

ous accident that cost him a leg. He had stopped his wagon at a gate, climbed down and opened the gate. While climbing back into the wagon seat, the horses spooked and ran away, with Hartman's leg stuck between the spokes. His leg got seriously mangled before he was able to stop the wagon, and it was amputated with a de-horning saw, the patient anesthetized with only whiskey.

In 1912, Hartman sold his Maher ranch of 1,550 acres - 700 acres in alfalfa - and 1,800 head of cattle, but later lost his fortune to failed investments in the mining industry and bad timing on cattle investments - the "buy high, sell low" syndrome. The final blow came with the failure of the Bank of Hotchkiss.

Hartman gave the last of his dwindling funds to families in Hotchkiss who had lost all they had in the bank failure.

JOHN McEVOY PHOTO

Cattle remain the traditional underpinning of the economy and lifestyle of the Crawford country.

Another legendary cattleman was John D. "Diamond Joe" Morrisey, who preceded Hartman in the Crawford country. Morrisey is described by Mamie Ferrier as "a tall, dark, and handsome man with a handlebar mustache and a Spanish look to his face. He was never seen without a pistol on his hip and a carbine in a scabbard hanging from his saddle. He sat straight in the saddle, had good fast horses, and could ride like the wind when he had to, to head off those long-winded long-horned cattle that could run like deer."

Morrisey was a "sooner," one who came to the Crawford country before the land was officially opened for settlement. It was said that Morrisey, who came from the mining camps at Leadville flush with mining profits, never really knew how many cattle were on the Diamond Joe ranch. He simply put as many cattle on the range as he could get, fattened them on the natural grasses, and shipped the lot to Kansas City.

Morrisey, years later when he was almost broke, reportedly said, regarding his once great fortune: "I spent most of it on women, liquor and gambling, but the rest I wasted." By 1890 Morrisey, along with his era, had faded into obscurity and his ranch was sold for back taxes. The last of the Diamond Joe Longhorns, wild as elk, were finally shot by homesteaders moving onto Fruitland Mesa.

In Morrisey's day, cattle were run in the high country for summer grazing, where they spread out and found enough to eat. But when winter came the herds were driven down by snow and gathered in the valleys where they denuded the native range. Winter losses were as high as 20 percent, so the more cattle a rancher had, the better his chances of coming out with a sizable herd in the spring.

The last major "open range roundup" in the Crawford country was in 1893. Gradually, cattlemen came to govern the size of their herds according to what they could raise for winter feed themselves. The day of the "range miner" came to an end.

Edgar W. Gates was another entrepreneurial cattleman of the Crawford country who originally sought his fortune in the mining camp of Gothic, north of Crested Butte. Injured in a mine explosion, Gates lost his vision in one eye, but was nursed back to health by a man who had gained a modicum of medical experience in an army hospital. Gates eventually left Gothic and became an investor in the Crosset Lumber Company of Arkansas where he became wealthy.

"Cap" Gates came west again with two desires, to get into the cattle business and reward the man who had nursed him in Gothic. He realized both desires in Crawford where he established a cattle herd and found Alex Morrow, a blacksmith, the man who had helped him during his time of need. Gates made Morrow

It wasn't always easy finding the right mount!

The homestead cabin at the Bar X Bar Ranch on the Smith Fork with Velma and Wilma Ferrier.

CRAWFORD CHRONICLE LOST IN A POKER GAME

The Crawford Chronicle was established around 1907 by Billy Hopkins of Paonia. The first newspaper office was in a stone house on the town's main street. The paper changed hands a number of times, but in 1910 it changed hands over a poker game.

The owner at the time was flush with money earned in mining at Crested Butte. In a poker game, while he was handicapped by a surplus of liquor, the man lost his stake. On a final bet, he offered the Chronicle, and lost that, too. The lucky winner went to the bank the next morning to see what his winnings were worth. When the banker told the new owner of the debts owed by the newspaper, the new owner promptly returned the paper to the previous owner, the big loser of the night before.

a partner in the Gates and Morrow Land and Cattle Company which Gates financed and Morrow ran.

The company came into possession of considerable land thanks to the Crawford country's first "mobile home." This was a cabin on wheels that Gates hauled from quarter section to quarter section, paying a cowboy to live in it until the land proved up. The temporary owner then would sell at a bargain price to Gates. Morrow died in 1914, and Gates and his sons continued with the enterprise until the 1920s, when they sold out and moved to the east with their considerable earnings.

Many cowboys in the early days rode herd over Black Mesa to the railhead at Sapinero. It was the lucky man who got to ride the train with the herd to the stock-yards in Denver or Kansas City. Each cowboy got the chance to see Denver or Kansas City, the honor being passed around so that everyone in the outfit got to "see the elephant."

Cowboys were known to celebrate once the herd was delivered. Crawford native Mamie Ferrier tells of a chilly night near Sapinero where a cowboy got so drunk he felt warmed all over and took off his boots, propped his feet up on a fence rail for the moon to warm, and passed out. His buddies, also somewhat inebriated, dragged him into the cow camp cabin, but when he failed to revive they thought he was dead. They dragged him out again and dumped him in the creek. When this failed to revive him, they opted for a burial.

The Night Riders

Chilled by their foray to the creek, they burned the dead man's boots for warmth in the stove. Then, for some reason, they rolled their friend's body in flour. Before last rites could be given, they too passed out. In the morning, all three awoke, and the hapless cowboy who had cheated death made the ride back to Crawford with stocking feet, no hat and dried flour stuck all over him.

When the Forest Homestead Act of 1913 subdivided the open range into farms and ranches, the once-free grazing rights enjoyed by cattlemen were cut short by strings of barbed wire. This,

Needle Rock, east of Crawford, is a weathered volcanic neck and a distinctive landmark of the Crawford Country.

CAROL CRAVEN PHOTO

Sheep and cattle didn't mix in the Crawford country when cattlemen held the open range. Today they do.

along with overgrazing and fluctuating, uncertain beef prices weakened the cattle industry in rural western Colorado. In its place came sheep.

Enos Hotchkiss, the namesake of the town of Hotchkiss, was one of the first to bring sheep to the North Fork Valley and environs in 1890. The cattlemen didn't like it, but they tolerated the old pioneer and his disdainful imports. But when others brought in more sheep, the competition for grazing land created a war.

When cattlemen claimed sheep ruined the range for their livestock, a vigilante force emerged to evict the sheep and sheepherders from the range.

The Cattleman's Protection Agency was formed to look after the interests of cattle growers. This group spawned the "Night Riders".

The Riders terrorized sheepherders with violence. The Night Riders came from other localities where sympathetic ranchers were asked to deal with the sheep problem away from their own homes.

Gradually, cattlemen lost ground and their herds shrunk. Sheep and cattle were regulated on the public range and the conflicts died away. Still, the Night Riders spoke to a possessiveness of the land and a rigid tradition that attempted to defy change in a rapidly changing West.

Crawford Reservoir

A mile south of Crawford, the Smith Fork Project, or Crawford Reservoir, was developed in 1960 as a means of storing high-water runoff. Spring runoff is a tumul-

tuous event where the high mountain snowpack melts rapidly, swelling rivers and streams with inordinately high water. This surge can create havoc for low lying areas. Conversely, autumn is a low-water season. Mountain reservoirs are built to even out the seasonal flows.

The Smith Fork Project was a modest $12 million dam and canal system designed to irrigate hay meadows and farming operations on the outlying mesas near Crawford. It was created by the Colorado River Storage Project for the Upper Basin of the Colorado, an Act passed by Congress in 1956.

Dam construction took two years of around-the-clock labor for the 195-feet-high earth-fill dam, requiring two million yards of packed dirt, mostly scraped from the site of the reservoir. A million yards of concrete were used to form the structure and mechanisms of the dam. Rock for the

Early transportation in the Crawford country was reliant upon the Crawford Stage.

Crawford Reservoir was completed in 1963 and provides storage for irrigation. Now the reservoir is a major recreation area for boating and fishing.

MAMIE FERRIER PHOTO

BUREAU OF RECLAMATION PHOTO

facing of the dam - a million and a half tons - was blasted from basalt cliffs at the edge Crawford.

The blast required 20 tons of dynamite loaded into a 40-foot tunnel dug into a cliff. The detonation shook the town and repairmen spent the rest of the day restoring electric and phone service.

The dam was dedicated on April 20, 1963. In attendance were key figures in the conservation and water storage development programs of the day; Secretary of Interior Stewart Udall, Commissioner of Reclamation Floyd Dominy and Colorado's Western Slope Congressman, Wayne Aspinall, "Mr. Chairman" of the House Interior Committee.

The Smith Fork Project opened an additional 1,400 acres of undeveloped land for cultivation and provided late summer irrigation for 8,000 acres already under irrigation. Today the reservoir is a popular, year-round recreation site that attracts more than 100,000 visitors annually to boat, fish, camp, hike, hunt, and swim.

POINTS OF INTEREST

Paonia Reservoir to Crawford. 37 miles

Highway 133 west from Paonia Dam follows the North Fork of the Gunnison River through a winding canyon studded with coal mines, opeining into the fertile North Fork Valley from Paonia to Hotchkiss.

- Mine reclamation at West Elk Mine, miles 21 and 18
- Historic mines visible to mile 9 at Paonia
- Somerset, historic coal mining town and operating mine, mile 18.
- Railroad tracks visible to Hotchkiss, mile 0; in early times Somerset was the only town known to exist in the US where rail was the only access, as no road existed.
- Fire Mountain canal, mile 17, brought irrigation water to the orchards.
- Bowie turnoff, Hubbard Creek, mile 16. Access to Grand Mesa, largest flat-top mountain in the world. Part of the Escalante Trail, the 1776 exploration and mapping of today's Colorado.
- Paonia information center, entrance to Paonia, mile 9. Information panels are here.
- Miner's memorial statue, honoring area men who died in the mines.
- North Fork Historical museum complex includes farm house and the original Bowie school.
- Dominguez-Escalante expedition marker, mile 4, commemorates the 1776 exploration party.
- Hotchkiss, mile 1; the second of the two fruit growing communities. Museum is located here.
- Turn south onto Highway 92 for Crawford, Black Canyon and Blue Mesa reservoir, mile 0.

Black Canyon and Blue Mesa

The Black Canyon of the Gunnison

The Crawford country spreads across the lower aspects of the sloping ramp of the Gunnison Uplift. The ramp climbs gradually southward and up to the precipitous rim of one of the greatest gorges in the west.

One mile south of Crawford Reservoir is the turn off to the North Rim of the Black Canyon of the Gunnison, the most dramatic geologic feature on the West Elk Loop. An 11-mile road (five miles are unpaved) climbs through ranching country into scrub oak, pinon, juniper and sagebrush hills that characterize vast portions of the dry Western Slope. The road ends at the North Rim of the canyon.

The canyon was, and still is, being carved at about one inch per century by the Gunnison River. The 2,000 feet deep canyon has been carved during the last two million years. The Black Canyon is prominent because the Gunnison established its stream bed on hard, Precambrian granite that was later pushed up by the Gunnison Uplift.

The river was channeled there originally by topmost layers of softer volcanic rock deposited from San Juan and West Elk volcanoes. Once the river began cutting into the Precambrian, it was there to stay. Surface water eventually eroded the softer shales surrounding the hard

JOHN MCEVOY

The deep gorge of the Black Canyon was carved over millions of years by the Gunnison River as it eroded Precambrian rock. That process continues today.

canyon rim, leaving it higher than the adjacent country.

Early explorers found their routes west blocked by this chasm. Ferdinand Hayden and his expedition of 1873-74, while making an extensive survey of mineral potential in western Colorado, determined there was no reasonable way through this rugged country for a transcontinental railroad, pronouncing it "inaccessible." A similar report had come from Captain John Gunnison in 1853.

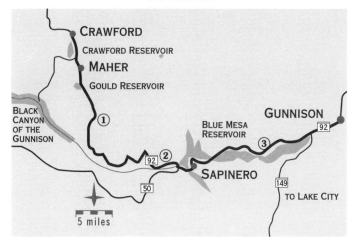

CRAWFORD TO GUNNISON
66 MILES

1. Crystal Creek
2. Pioneer Point
3. Elk Creek Marina

The gorge is 53 miles long and 1,800 to over 2,660 feet deep. Twelve miles of the deepest, most breathtaking portion of canyon are preserved as the Black Canyon of the Gunnison National Monument. A large portion of the canyon east of the Monument is traversed by the curving, winding Highway 92, one of Colorado's most spectacular rim highways.

Wildlife along the canyon rim includes chipmunks, ground squirrels, weasels, badgers, marmots, black bear, bobcat and cougars. Coyotes are heard at night, and mule deer are a common sight. Porcupines leave their marks on gnawed trees, and a large variety of birds, from hummingbirds to bald eagles, call the area home. Rainbow and German brown trout are found in the pools of the river. Rock climbers frequent the vertical walls.

On March 2, 1933, due to efforts of citizens in Montrose who desired the canyon's preservation, President Herbert Hoover proclaimed the Black Canyon of the Gunnison a National Monument. Since then, a portion of the canyon has been designated Wilderness to preserve its wild character and to ensure that the landscape will remain forever in its natural state.

Laying Rails in the Black Canyon

Despite the Black Canyon's intimidating depth and the snarling rapids of the Gunnison River, which at one point plummets beneath a plug of house-sized boulders, the canyon was challenged by surveyors who entered in search of a railroad route and later by a daring duo

From the south rim of the Black Canyon, spectacular views offer visitors a glance into the 2,000-foot deep gorge and a view across to the north rim where the access road from Crawford leads.

who navigated the river searching for a water diversion to the parched Uncompahgre Valley.

Described as impassable by Rio Grande engineers in 1880, William Jackson Palmer, owner of the railroad, overruled their findings and launched another survey in 1881. Men, horses and wagons were lowered into the canyon by ropes. After that final survey Palmer ordered the rail pushed through the same summer. In more than a year of incredible labor, railroad builders created the 15-mile stretch of "impossible" track from Sapinero to Cimarron. The track passed the towering Curecanti Needle, which became the symbol of the Rio Grande on its "Scenic Line of the World" logo.

Laying rails through the canyon is one of the most incredible tales of pluck and perseverance in railroad history. Irish and Italian crews, 1,000 men, blasted and cut with picks and shovel, a shelf above the frothing Gunnison River. They built bridges and defied rational limits as they pursued their mission.

They worked through the winter of 1881-82 when the sun rarely touched the depths of the canyon and temperatures often dropped below zero. Theirs is an epic tale of hardship and danger that demonstrates the relentless drive of the railroaders.

The men braved rockfalls and avalanches, killing cold and the torrents of the river to establish the "road." They lived in a "hotel" train which followed their progress and provided a full kitchen and sleeping quarters. The work was miserable and demanding, but an account from the time illustrates that the challenge was taken with pride and a rarely seen human strength. A journalist who followed the construction detailed the hunger with which men approached the dining table at day's end, the desperate conditions with which they lived and, above it all, their incredible resilience.

"It was a glimpse of a hard cheerless life that I had had, but as I turned to go back to the construction train some one struck up a rollicking Irish song and others joined until the canyon walls gave back the chorus."

One of the hazards came from working with a "nasty" liquid explosive called nitroglycerine. On August 11, 1881, a crew was blasting the grade just west of Sapinero at the entrance to the Black Canyon when a nitro charge went off prematurely. One man was blown into the Gunnison River, his body disappearing beneath a rock fall. A "Negro grader" had his head, left shoulder and side mangled by flying rock. He died an hour later. Another grader, standing just as close, was blown 50 feet away and was unharmed. Another man had an arm blown off.

An ethnic clash occurred in the Black Canyon on October 9, 1881 when an Irishman bet an Italian grading foreman, Mike Soso, that he couldn't drink an entire bottle of whiskey. Soso took the bet and drank the bottle, but became so inebriated that he went into a rage, pulled a knife and stabbed an Irish bystander. The remaining Irishmen took flight, pursued by Italians firing at them.

That night, a strong contingent of Irish marched on the Italian camp to arrest Soso. After an exchange of gunfire, in which no one was injured, they

The Black Canyon is impressive whether viewed from river level or from the rims.

apprehended the Italian. The Italian camp then mounted a force and marched upon the Irish camp to free the prisoner. The mob was stopped by a railroad contractor who agreed to release Soso. The mob disbanded.

The following morning, the same contractor approached the Italian camp to get the men to work. He was met by another hostile mob of Italians who threatened to kill him if they weren't immediately paid off in full. The contractor refused a settlement until payday and retreated to the Irish camp. The angry Italians followed, but were met by 50 armed Irishmen who chased them back to their camp, scattering the mob. Some of the Italians headed for the hills; others jumped into the Gunnison River. Thirty Italians were captured and disarmed. Some of their tents were set afire.

With tensions high, another incident occurred October 27 when an Italian speaking Austrian nipper (tool carrier) named Theophile walked into the office of the contractor, Colonel Hoblitzell, and demanded his wages. Hoblitzell refused, saying he required a 10-day notice. When Theophile continued badgering him, Hoblitzell attempted to usher him from the office.

A fight ensued, with Theophile reportedly taking the worst of it. The fight was broken up, but Theophile drew a gun and shot Hoblitzell point blank in the chest.

Hoblitzell staggered back into his office while Theophile ran off, threatening anyone who might interfere. W. P. Coghill, the storekeeper, rode off to Gunnison for a doctor and made the 22 miles in under two hours. Hoblitzell remained conscious, even though the bullet had penetrated his chest, and his wife and daughter were notified of the shooting and sent for from Colorado Springs. A posse began a fruitless search for Theophile, and a wanted poster was printed in Gunnison offering $1000 for his capture.

Hoblitzell died at 9 p.m. while his wife and daughter were enroute by rail

A Rio Grande train steams along the Gunnison River deep in the Black Canyon, the vision of a bygone era.

somewhere on the east side of Marshall Pass. Sheriff George Yule arrived an hour before the victim's death and began a search with two deputies. They found Theophile the next morning standing at a campfire holding a dead

Monument management assistant Dave Roberts takes a look at the Black Canyon from the precarious rim.

rabbit and his shotgun. They disarmed and arrested him.

Feelings for revenge were high at the grading camps as the sheriff, riding Theophile double behind him, passed through. "Stop. Bring the son of a bitch here! Give him to us!" yelled some of the crew. The sheriff and deputies spurred their horses and reached Gunnison without incident. There Theophile was shackled upstairs in the courthouse and guarded for safekeeping.

That night, a dozen men bearing cocked pistols and wearing black masks marched in with a rope and found the prisoner sleeping on a bench.

The masked men slipped the rope around Theophile's neck and dragged

him down the stairs. Theophile screamed and choked as the vigilantes dragged him away. The trail in the snow led to a livery stable on Tomichi Avenue [U.S. Highway 50]. The bloodied, bruised corpse of Theophile was hanging from the livery stable sign. It appeared that the Austrian was dead even before the hanging.

The Gunnison *News-Democrat* decried the vigilante killing as a travesty of justice perpetrated by the railroad workers. "Good God, has it come to this, that a railroad monopoly can override all the business of law and order which a respectable city has created for its own protection?"

Despite such conflicts and dramas, the crews reached Cimarron on August 9, 1882, where 27 railroad "hotels" lined the sidings, a moving city of working men. A Rio Grande excursion train carrying 121 people from Gunnison made the first passenger trip through the canyon on August 13, 1882. Palmer had spent $165,000 a mile getting the train to Cimarron, and still the train had to push over rugged Cerro Summit into the Uncompahgre Valley.

Once the line was up and running, the Black Canyon posed a major threat to Rio Grande engineers who traveled the line. A railroaders' hell, the canyon was responsible for many deaths from avalanches and rock slides.

Rudyard Kipling traveled the Rio Grande line over Marshall Pass and through the Black Canyon in 1889. He wrote: "There was a glory and a wonder and a mystery about the mad ride which I felt keenly."

The Byron Bryant Party

Despite Palmer's success in reaching Cimarron and conquering part of the canyon, he wasn't satisfied. Determined to discover a more direct route through the heart of the Black Canyon, in 1882 he commissioned the Byron Bryant party to survey the remainder of the canyon which until then could be viewed only from the rims.

The Bryant party entered the canyon just before Christmas in 1882, expecting to complete the task in 20 days. In less than 20 days, however, all but five members of the expedition had quit because of harsh conditions and grave personal risk. A mid-winter exploration of the canyon staggers the imagination, as the men had to forge through deep snows and across icy rocks in their efforts.

The five men who completed the survey took 68 days to plumb the canyon's depths and traverse its length. They climbed into the canyon every morning and back out again to base camps at night. Bryant's conclusion to Palmer indicated the impossibility of building "anything" in the further reaches of the Black Canyon.

Torrence and Fellows: Canyon Odyssey

In 1901 another survey team entered the canyon to survey a water diversion project, the Gunnison Tunnel, which would carry water from the Gunnison River into the parched Uncompahgre Valley.

A survey was required to determine if the level of the Gunnison River was high enough to generate a flow, and it was undertaken by William Torrence and Abraham Lincoln Fellows. Unlike the Bryant party, which operated from base camps on the rim, Torrence and Fellows penetrated the length of the canyon floor in a heroic, life threatening journey.

Fellows was a hydrographer for the U.S. Geological Survey who first came to Colorado in 1887. He took the assignment in 1901 and advertised in nearby Montrose for an engineer and assistant who must be "a strong swimmer, unmarried, temperate, and obedient." William Torrence of Montrose was his man.

Torrence knew the canyon, having advanced 14 miles beyond the Cimarron River on a failed expedition the previous year. On that journey, Torrence had learned that a successful expedition must rely not on heavy boats and a burden of supplies, but on a light craft and light gear, easy to portage around the huge rapids and giant boulders.

The men set off in August 1901 when water levels were low, determined to go the distance. They would be supplied occasionally from above, and they entered the gorge at Cimarron with a small raft, two 600-foot silk ropes, backpacks and rubber bags for food. For days they swam, rafted and hiked down the canyon. They met one resupply, then ventured where none had gone before. Fellows described his feelings when he saw "the mighty jaws, past which there was to be no escape. I believe I might be pardoned for the feeling of nervousness and dread which came over me for the first time."

Those "jaws" were The Narrows at the Falls of Sorrow, which had turned back Torrence in his previous expedition. The two men could see a giant bonfire in the canyon beyond where their faithful and equally daring support man, A. W. Dillon, was waiting for them. There was only one way to proceed. Boldly, Torrence, then Fellows, dove into the vapor-spewing rapids. Miraculously, they made it through the falls and met Dillon.

Beyond The Narrows was an even more challenging section where huge boulders, worn smooth by the river, completely blocked the channel. Unable to float the river or climb the boulders, the explorers were forced to traverse the sheer canyon wall.

It took them six hours to travel less than a quarter mile as they clambered through giant rocks and swam across frothing pools, which the river brought to the surface only to suck back underground between the rocks.

Fellows was caught in one of these whirlpools and nearly pulled beneath the surface. At one point the boulders became too polished, and the walls of the canyon too vertical and sheer to climb around.

There was no retreat, so the men, standing at the edge of a whirlpool, steeled themselves. Fellows went first, leaping into the black, swirling water.

Torrance watched as his partner was pulled down into the vortex, swept below to an uncertain fate. Torrance paused a moment in uncertainty, and it staggers the mind to appreciate his conundrum. Then, taking a deep breath, he leaped, joining his partner in whatev-

Rock climbers in the Black Canyon are dwarfed by the enormity of the canyon walls, the same walls that challenged surveyors Bryant, Torrence and Fellows.

er the churning suck-hole might conspire. The men were flushed beneath the boulders for 25 feet by the turbulent river, banged into rocks, and spit out the other side. They suffered only scrapes and bruises.

Out of food and sickened from the ordeal the men were still far from their next resupply. Luckily, they surprised two mountain sheep, one of which got spooked from a ledge and broke its shoulder in a fall. The men made a meal out of a hindquarter and sustained enough nourishment to continue their journey. They met Dillon at another resupply point, and although thoughts of leaving the canyon were entertained, the men had caught the "fever" of exploration. They determined to go on.

Then came the longest, toughest day of their journey, traveling the canyon depths for many hours. As dusk fell that night they camped without bedding, their clothes soaked, and with no food. They were ill from exertion, cold and a lack of sleep. Both adventurers had lost considerable weight. The next day they called it quits and hiked out on a horse trail toward Delta. Their survey proved that a diversion tunnel could be built in the canyon. It also secured a place for Torrence and Fellows in Colorado history.

The Gunnison Tunnel

With passage of the Newlands Act of 1902, the federal government became an advocate and financial partner for water projects in the arid West. The Reclamation Department was created to build irrigation schemes to water parched western lands and reclaim the cost of those ventures through assessments on the newly irrigated land.

The Uncompahgre Valley on Colorado's Western Slope became a pilot project for the new agency. Once the Torrence and Fellows survey showed that the elevation of the

President William Howard Taft receives a gold bell to ring as a signal for the opening of the Gunnison Tunnel on September 23, 1909. The tunnel diverted water from the Gunnison River to the Uncompahgre Valley.

Gunnison River where it cascades through the Black Canyon of the Gunnison was high enough to reach the Uncompahgre Valley, the Reclamation Department began building the Gunnison Tunnel in 1905.

A work force of hundreds of men labored from both portals on the 5.9-mile tunnel beneath Vernal Mesa. Access to the east portal was achieved on a harrowing 12-mile wagon road traversing the great drop of the canyon with frightful 22% grades. For four years the workers bored beneath the Mesa, encountering fractured, unstable rock, underground rivers and hot water seams.

Conditions were so dangerous and the work so difficult that despite good pay and benefits from the contractor, Taylor -

Moore Construction of Hillsboro, Texas, the average stay for a worker was just two weeks. Six men were killed during construction, and the cost of the tunnel soared to more than $10 million.

On September 23, 1909, President William Howard Taft presided at the opening of the Gunnison Tunnel, a lifeline to the Uncompahgre Valley that, despite all the promise, brought mixed results. Much of the land intended for irrigation proved alkaline and unsuitable for crops; the diversion didn't produce as much water as initially expected; and with the high costs of construction user fees had to be adjusted several times. Still, the project, the first federally funded water project in Colorado, set a major precedent.

Caleb Maher.

The Caleb Maher home, with Maher seated.

Maher

A small collection of buildings on Highway 92 south of the Black Canyon access road is the townsite of Maher. The town is named for Caleb Maher, its founder, who settled there in the early 1880s and decided to petition for a post office. To do so, Maher walked to Gunnison, filed his petition and walked back again, a 140-mile trek.

Maher, a farming and ranching community, was never much more than is visible today. It had a post office until the 1980s, and it had a school. The first schoolhouse was built in 1885 and was made of cedar posts standing on end with a dirt roof. In 1917 the existing schoolhouse was built. It is used today as the Maher Community Center and club house. School was held there until 1950, when children were bussed to Crawford.

Gould Reservoir

Gould Reservoir, south of Maher, can be credited as much to naivete as remarkable ingenuity. The project was immense for a private undertaking when it was conceived in 1901 by the Gould family. They had been encouraged to invest in the water diversion for the dry Fruitland Mesa plateau by a Dutch colony that came west from Iowa. These settlers wanted to raise fruit, settle down, rear their families, speak Dutch, and worship in the Dutch Reformed Church. Most were relatives of John Sipman who was foreman of the Gould Reservoir and Ditch project.

Originally from Nebraska, the Gould brothers, Jim, Ernest, John and George, had prospered in Aspen during its mining heyday. But as the boom turned to bust with the collapse of silver in 1893, the brothers sought a joint venture. They

decided to develop the water project to irrigate a large section of land they owned on the Smith Fork. They named it the Fruitland Mesa project.

The only water the Goulds had been able to tap for their land came from Crystal Creek which was fully allotted by then except during high-water runoff in the spring. A dam would have to be built, plus a network of ditches to transport water once it was captured. The Goulds conceived a plan to build a reservoir, and the brothers were joined by their father, Willard Gould, who came from Nebraska to assist his sons with organizational and logistical details.

The Goulds sold shares to finance the project, which was estimated at $200,000. To house the construction crew they built a tent city including a dining hall, bunkhouses, family tents and commissary. They built a sawmill to provide lumber

MAMIE FERRIER

In the early days of the Crawford country roads were narrow and one lane. The "Kraii Grade" out of the Smith Fork Canyon was built by Dutch settlers. It later connected to Black Mesa and became Highway 92, part of the West Elk Loop Scenic Byway.

Gould reservoir was a huge undertaking when it was begun in 1901 by the Gould family who sought to irrigate Fruitland Mesa.

and employed a dozen draft teams and the largest steam tractor to come to the Crawford country at the time to clear the mesa of pinon and juniper.

Their plan was to utilize a hydraulic dam-building technique similar to that used in hydraulic mining. To gain sufficient water pressure, the Goulds built the Fruitland Highline Ditch high above the proposed dam. The water was funneled down to a four inch nozzle fixed on a wooden platform, providing considerable pressure. The stream of water was then directed at a hillside near the dam, and the force of the water eroded the slope. The earthen fill, in a slurry, was carried in a wooden flume nearly a quarter mile to the dam.

Since the Goulds were restricted to high-water runoff for their project, their water supply was available only in the spring. As a result, the dam required three years to reach 45 feet. Meanwhile, two tunnels, one a quarter mile, the other half a mile, were dug to carry the impounded water from the reservoir to Fruitland Mesa. Two large siphons were needed, one 30 inches and the other 20 inches in diameter. They were made from wooden staves banded with half-inch iron.

Mrs. Juanita Cotton was head cook for most of the project years. The commissary furnished the bare necessities - overalls for 50 cents, shoes for $1.50, shirts from 45 to 90 cents, and beef for 6 1/2 cents a pound. Wages were 25 cents an hour for a 10-hour day. Room and board were $1 a day.

As construction expenses mounted, however, the Goulds faced bankruptcy and sought Eastern investors. By 1910, the project was completed, though an

Horse packing was the first means of entering the Crawford country. Clint Ferrier leads a string across a precarious boulder field.

Black Mesa was a major obstacle for settlers entering the Crawford Country and North Fork Valley, but it provided timber for building and grazing land for cattle. Grant Ferrier skids a log with two horsepower.

additional 15 feet was later added to the dam height.

Unfortunately for the Goulds, Fruitland Mesa was not the cornucopia they had envisioned. The 1,500-foot difference in elevation above the North Fork Valley meant a later fruit crop, so by the time their harvest came, the fruit markets were already glutted. Rabbits and deer wreaked havoc on the fruit trees, and the high-water runoff was not always dependable. In low snow years, there might be only 15 or 20 days of irrigation water available. Frosts also hampered fruit growing.

The Goulds lost financially in the venture, but in the end they succeeded in capitalizing a substantial project through the private sector and in benefiting a portion of the Crawford country with the blessing of water.

Black Mesa

As Highway 92 makes the gradual incline toward the rim of the Black Canyon, it passes Crystal River Road, the original route into the Crawford country over Black Mesa, a thickly timbered mountain. The old road traverses above the current highway and climbs through scrub oak, aspen, and spruce forests.

Early settlers came over Black Mesa, as did Crawford country rancher Sam Hartman, who crossed "the Black" with herds of cattle to and from Sapinero in the 1880s, following the old Ute Indian trail. Pioneers followed Hartman's route and trimmed it as they went, but the grades were so steep that it often took three teams of horses to negotiate them. In some places, sidehills required riders

to rope off wagons from the high side to keep them from tipping. Wagon drivers sometimes tied huge spruce logs to their wagons as drag anchors to control speed on the steep descents.

The trip was so arduous for wagon drivers that they sometimes rested for a week or two at the top to let themselves and their teams recover. One pioneer family heading to the Crawford country made it "over the Black," then stopped in Onion Valley to boil water, wash, get the men shaved, and put on clean clothes before entering the "new country."

Black Mesa was a major source of timber for the Crawford area, and it was logged for many years. When logging came under Forest Service jurisdiction, the cuts were highly selective. A ranger cruised the forests selecting over-mature

Blue Mesa Reservoir, spanned by U.S. Highway 50, covers the townsites of Sapinero, Iola, Kezar and Cebolla along the Rio Grande's Scenic Line of the World. The largest body of water in Colorado, Blue Mesa's excellent fishing and 96 miles of shoreline attract boaters, fishermen and campers.

Sapinero

Submerged beneath hundreds of feet of Blue Mesa Reservoir lie the remnants of Sapinero, a town built at the entrance to the Black Canyon and which in 1881 served as an end-of-the-line camp on the Rio Grande railroad line. The town was first called Soap Creek, for a nearby drainage, but was changed to Sapinero in honor of a sub-chief of the Utes, a brother-in-law to Chief Ouray.

Sapinero was a transportation hub on the Rio Grande's Gunnison - Cimarron line and as the terminus for the Lake City extension, a spur begun in 1881 but not completed until 1889. Freight roads went to Powderhorn, Barnum and Ouray, and Sapinero became a major supply center featuring two hotels, the Rainbow and the Sapinero, plus a mercantile store.

As a railhead Sapinero was frequented by cowboys from the Crawford Country who drove their herds over Black Mesa and loaded them into cattle cars. The cattle were shipped through Gunnison, over Marshall Pass, then on to slaughter houses in Denver or Kansas City. The cowboys celebrated many successful drives in Sapinero which may account for a description by a Gunnison *News-Democrat* reporter in 1883:

"I found a fact which would go far to upset the theories of the Prohibitionists ... that the people of Soap Creek live on whiskey. There is no other visible means of living, as among eight or nine saloons, [only] one combines the business of a restaurant."

As railroad construction crews moved on to Cimarron, Sapinero lost some of its

and diseased trees and stamping them with a U.S. Forest Service blaze, low on the trunk. Loggers made certain not to leave any stumps without the Forest Service blaze.

There were some large clearcuts on Black Mesa in the 1950s that have not yet grown back despite numerous plantings of a variety of evergreens. Those large cuts, it is argued, did a disservice to the small, local loggers who were unable to bid on large contracts against the big timber companies.

The first district ranger on Black Mesa was Benjamin Heilman who served as a ranger from 1906 to 1933. With 23 of those years on "the Black", Heilman had

an effective and diplomatic management style that won over the local loggers. After he retired, Heilman made the Black Mesa rounds with his younger replacements. In old age he requested to be buried there. A simple bronze marker at Curecanti Creek reveals the grave site.

The Black Mesa road is little traveled even today, although Highway 92 is one of the most scenic roads in the state, with striking views into the Black Canyon and south to the San Juan Mountains. Highway 92 ends just beyond Blue Mesa dam at U.S. Highway 50 where the West Elk Loop turns east along Blue Mesa Reservoir toward Gunnison.

economic base. Still, it remained a supply center for outlying areas and served as a jumping off place for the Crawford country until the 1890s, when the railroad reached the North Fork Valley via an easier route through Delta.

During the Depression, in 1932 the famed Civil War author Bruce Catton visited Sapinero with his wife and a nephew, where they had a frightening experience on the railroad line. The Cattons were out for a stroll and were returning to Sapinero when they crossed the railroad trestle and were surprised halfway across by a Rio Grande engine bearing down on them. Jumping 100 feet to jagged rocks below was out of the question, and Catton described how they evaded the engine:

"Fortunately, the thirty feet or so of the mid-section of this trestle had over-length ties ...and a four-by-four stringer lay on top of them, parallel with the rail ... Somehow we managed to lie down on the tie ends outside of the stringer, hugging same with our left arms, with our right arms and legs sort of floating off in space. ... That train looked as big and as ominous as the Broadway Limited. Not to keep you in suspense, we had plenty of clearance and were not knocked off into the gulch; the train passed, we rolled to the left, got to our feet, and tottered feebly to the end of the trestle and safety."

Today's Sapinero is merely a gas stop on the east side of the highway a mile or so east of Blue Mesa dam. A new village of summer homes and cabins is clustered on a hillside across the Lake Fork of the reservoir.

The Rainbow Hotel of Sapinero was one of two hotels in the thriving railroad town in 1884. First called Soap Creek, Sapinero was renamed for the brother-in-law of Ute Indian Chief Ouray. The townsite is submerged beneath Blue Mesa Reservoir.

The Beautiful Gunnison

Before Blue Mesa Reservoir filled the Gunnison River Valley 10 miles west of the city of Gunnison, the Gunnison River was reputed to be one of the best trout streams in the U.S., perhaps the world. Fisherman and hunters frequented resort communities built along the river banks and the railroad. The little communities of Iola, Kezar, Cebolla and Sapinero were favorite destinations. Trout were plentiful and so was big game.

Iola, ten miles west of Gunnison, just beyond the meanders of the Gunnison Canyon, was created by cattleman A. K.

Stevens in 1896. It had a small log schoolhouse, general store and post office. Iola also had hotels to serve the vacationing sportsman - the Rio Vista Resort, Wilt Hotel, Zeigler Hotel and the Iola Hotel.

The town experienced a dramatic event in 1910 when L. E. Champlin, a storekeeper at Powderhorn, shot and killed his employer, Mat Cavanaugh, at the Iola Post Office. There had been bad feelings between the men, and a few days before the shooting, Cavanaugh had broken his rifle stock over Champlin's head at Powderhorn, knocking him unconscious. At Iola, fearing violence from his enemy,

Before Blue Mesa Reservoir flooded 20 miles of the Gunnison River Valley, fishermen referred to its clear waters as some of the best trout fishing waters in the world.

Champlin fired three shots into the advancing Cavanaugh. Cavanaugh died, but the shooting was ruled self-defense, and Champlin never went to trial.

Iola was a rail center for cattle pools in the area, and many thousands of head were shipped on the Rio Grande. Copper and gold ore from the mines at Vulcan and Spencer, and from the Powderhorn-Cebolla region, were also shipped from Iola. A mile west of Iola was the small town of Kezar, named for Gardner Kezar, who filed a plat on the location in 1881.

Kezar rose to prominence and was even suggested as being likely to displace Gunnison for its strategic and scenic location. According to the Gunnison Review, the town "...is destined to become a great place of resort, nestled as it is in a circular park surrounded by hills and mountains, which, together with its river, its islands and meadows, seems more like a gem ... an emerald set in a border of pure gold."

By spring of 1882, Kezar had five saloons, four general stores, two boarding houses and a dance hall. But the boom was short-lived. That year the Rio Grande moved its terminus toward Cimarron and most of the population followed. The town struggled for existence, but 20 years later only a railroad section house remained.

Cebolla was located alongside the Rio Grande tracks midway between Sapinero and Kezar and was founded by J. J. Carpenter, a rancher from North Carolina. Carpenter built the renowned Sportsman Lodge at Cebolla (which is Spanish for onion), a wild variety of which grew in profusion along Cebolla creek. The Sportsman Lodge burned down in 1902, but was quickly rebuilt to serve a steady clientele of fishermen and hunters.

Iola, Kezar and Cebolla met the same fate as Sapinero when they were flooded by Blue Mesa Reservoir in the early 1960s. The resorts, the Rio Grande rail line, and the beautiful Gunnison itself were all submerged beneath more than 100 feet of water.

Curecanti National Recreation Area

Curecanti National Recreation Area, named for Curecata, a Ute Indian chief, is the largest of the recreational amenities on the West Elk Loop. Configured mostly around Blue Mesa Reservoir, which is the largest body of water in Colorado, Curecanti also includes three deep canyon dams in the upper end of the Black Canyon—Blue Mesa, Morrow Point and Crystal.

From Crystal Creek Trail (Mile 48.5) where Highway 92 begins its serpentine meanders headed north along the rim of the Black Canyon to Neversink on Highway 50, a mile east of the Lake City Bridge, the Curecanti National Recreation Area provides hiking, picnicking, boating, camping and a palpable sense of the region's history.

Managed by the National Park Service Curecanti bears the imprint of man attempting to alter the natural landscape. His success is marked by three major dams and three major lakes, the most popular of which is the 20-mile-long Blue Mesa Reservoir. The dam projects - officially named the Wayne N. Aspinall unit dams of the Bureau of Reclamation's Upper Colorado River Storage Project - impound the waters of the Gunnison for irrigation, hydroelectric energy and recreation. Aspinall was a long-time Western Slope Congressman from Colorado and Chair of the House Interior Committee who prodded the dam projects.

Blue Mesa, with 96 miles of shoreline, is a boater's haven that attracts sailing and powerboats. It is a fisherman's par-

LAKE CITY, WHERE THE GOLD RUSH STARTED

Lake City, on the edge of the San Juan Mountains, sprang into being because of Enos Hotchkiss when he and famed Colorado pioneer and road builder, Otto Mears, constructed a toll road from Saguache through the Gunnison Country and into the San Juans. Their timing was perfect as this mineral rich region had just opened to hordes of miners in 1873 as a result of the Brunot Treaty with the Ute Indians.

Mears began the project in answer to miners in the San Juans calling for a good road for shipping in supplies and hauling out ore. Mears forged a road over Marshall Pass into the Gunnison Country, then contracted the final section of the road to Enos Hotchkiss, who pushed the road up the Lake Fork of the Gunnison River.

While excavating the road on the perimeter of the San Juans, late in 1874, Hotchkiss uncovered a rich gold strike. According to *Crofutt's Gripsack Guide* of 1881, Hotchkiss's Golden Fleece produced "float rock" that assayed at $40,000 per ton. "It is one of the best developed mines and makes average runs up in the thousands." The mine was the first to open in the region, attracting much attention.

Hotchkiss quit road building and began to develop the Golden Fleece. Around him Lake City boomed in a matter of months. By 1875 the town had 67 buildings, 400 residents. and became Hinsdale County seat. By 1876 the population had more than doubled, with 2,000 miners roaming the nearby creeks and valleys. Six to twelve wagons arrived daily over the Saguache-San Juan toll road. As an early account reported, "Prospectors and townmakers flocked to the region, and Lake City developed a population of five thousand silver seekers in a matter of weeks."

The boom turned to bust in 1881, however, as the shipping costs to and from remote Lake City became prohibitive. Winters were long and hard and shut down many of the mines. When the Rio Grande abandoned it's Lake City connection in 1881 the town fell into a major depression. In 1889 an ambitious rail connection was finally completed between Sapinero and Lake City, and the mining town gained a new lease on life.

The rail line was epic in construction because of the Lake Fork canyon, which was comparable to the Black Canyon in the difficulty of establishing a road bed. An army of 700 Italian railroaders spread out along the grade blasting, picking and digging. Four miles of sheer canyon wall had to be blasted, and an 800-foot-long, 113-foot-high trestle was built with a million board feet of lumber to span the Lake Fork.

For Enos Hotchkiss, Lake City lost its appeal with the exhaustion of ore in the Golden Fleece. He lost heavily on the venture and reverted to hunting, which is what he knew best. He remained in the Lake City, and later in the Powderhorn area, and became the "champion mountain lion killer of the district," as one account credited him. "In one year he dispatched thirty-six of the predators, earning enough bounty and thanks of the besieged community to defray his disappointment at the early exhaustion of his mine." He moved on to found the town of Hotchkiss.

---

adise and even during the cold winter months, when temperatures can slip to 40 below zero, ice fishing and ice skating are popular activities.

Blue Mesa Dam , the first of the three dams built, was begun in 1962. The $42 million project provides water storage for irrigation, impounds 940,800 acre feet, recreation for a million annual visitors, and produces 87,000 kilowatts of electricity. The dam is 342-feet high.

Morrow Point Dam, 12 miles downstream, was completed in 1970 to hold water in the fjord-like Black Canyon itself. It produces the bulk of Curecanti's hydroelectric power-173,000 kilowatts. Impounding 117,000 acre feet of water, the towering 469-foot high concrete dam holds a deep reservoir that is popular with fishermen who cast for rainbow, German brown and brook trout and Kokanee salmon.

Morrow Point boat tours are regularly scheduled in the summer months on an excursion boat where passengers learn the history of the area and gaze at the sheer canyon walls and the famed Curecanti Needle from lake level. Reservations may be made through the Elk Creek Marina at Blue Mesa, or by calling (970) 641-0402.

Crystal Dam is six miles downstream from Morrow Point. Standing 357 feet high this concrete dam, completed in 1977 for $53 million, holds 26,000 acre feet of water, produces 28,000 kilowatts of energy, and regulates the flow of water through the Black Canyon of the The

Dillon Pinnacles is the weathered edge of a huge mud flow from the West Elk volcano that formed the West Elk Mountains. A hiking trail allows for a close-up view of the Pinnacles.

BUREAU OF RECLAMATION

Morrow Point Dam is 12 miles into the Black Canyon of the Gunnison. The generators there produce the bulk of the Curecanti project hydroelectric power. The dam is 469 feet high.

Gunnison National Monument, just downstream.

A hike along the Black Canyon rim on the Crystal Creek Trail (2.5 miles long) offers a vantage point of the reservoir 1,800 feet below. Hermit's Rest Trail (3 miles long) offers a strenuous hike to Morrow Point Reservoir, with lakeside camping available.

The Curecanti Creek Trail (2 miles long) descends from Pioneer Point to Morrow Point Reservoir. All three trails can be found along Highway 92 as it winds along the rugged canyon rim. Other trails of note on Highway 50 east of Blue Mesa Dam are the 2.5-mile-long Dillon Pinnacles Trail and the half mile Neversink Trail with its lush, streamside bird habitat.

Information centers are located at Lake Fork, near Blue Mesa Dam, and at Elk Creek where the National Park Service has its headquarters. A restaurant is also located at Elk Creek. There are several public campgrounds in the Curecanti area, with a wide variety of environments and backdrops. For information or reservations, contact the National Park Service, 102 Elk Creek, Gunnison, CO. 81230, or call (970) 641-2337.

The "Colorado Cannibal"

The most notorious and nefarious character ever to play a role in Gunnison history was Alferd Packer, the "Colorado Cannibal." Packer's role was a cameo, but it was as unsavory and sensational a role as one may imagine.

Originally from Pennsylvania, Packer served a brief stint in the Union Army in 1862. Plagued with epilepsy, he was discharged for physical disability and wandered the West, working as a ranch hand, guide, hunter and miner.

On November 21, 1873, Packer, then 42, joined 20 other prospectors determined to travel from Provo, Utah to the newly discovered gold fields of Breckenridge, which Packer said he was familiar with. By mid-January of 1874, the party had reached the camp of Chief Ouray near the present site of Delta where it was held up by snow. The chief advised the prospectors not to venture any farther until the weather had cleared.

Packer and five others - Wilson Bell, Frank Miller, Israel Swan, George Noon and James Humphreys - ignored the chief's advice and decided to skirt the snowbound San Juan Mountains toward the Los Pinos Agency 40 miles southeast of Gunnison.

The last eye witnesses, who were trapping on Dry Creek near present day Lake City, watched as the ill-fated party disappeared into a storm. There was no word from the prospectors until April 16, 1874 when Alferd Packer emerged alone from the wilderness at Los Pinos Agency, a

Alferd Packer, convicted of eating human flesh.

GUNNISON PIONEER MUSEUM

Winchester carbine slung over his shoulder. The exhausted Packer told of his going snow blind and being left in camp by his compatriots who forged ahead and never returned. Packer said he had been left some food and that he managed to struggle through. He seemed well fed and healthy and the first thing he asked for was whiskey, not food.

Packer's story was not uncommon for those days, as men were often getting lost and wandering aimlessly through the wilderness. The agency men thought little of it, and Packer left two days later for Saguache, where he aroused suspicion by spending money freely. He also possessed the rifle of one man from his party and the hunting knife of another. Otto Mears, then of Saguache, caught wind of the odd circumstances and induced the Los Pinos

Indian agent to question him. Packer was caught up in contradictions and made a first confession.

Packer said the party had gotten lost, used up its provisions, and that, as the men dropped off because of the fearful winter conditions, the others ate their flesh. Swan died first, then Humphreys, Packer said. Miller was accidentally killed, and he, too, was eaten. Finally, Bell shot Noon. Then Packer, in self defense, shot and killed Bell. He covered the remains and, packing a large piece of human flesh, walked 14 days to Los Pinos Agency. Packer admitted to have taken $133 off the body of Humphreys.

Packer was arrested on suspicion of homicide and jailed that summer of 1874 in Saguache. When the bodies of Packer's party-or what was left of them-were found in August, it became apparent that the men were murdered and dismembered, and that no struggle had taken place. The site, now marked by a shrine, is two miles south of present day Lake City on State Highway 149, just across the Lake Fork Bridge toward Slumgullion Pass.

Packer escaped from the Saguache jail before he could be brought to trial. Nearly ten years later, on March 12, 1883 he was recaptured in Wyoming, where he had been using the alias "John Schwartze." He was returned to Lake City to account for charges of murder and cannibalism, of which he was convicted. According to a report, supposedly by a newspaper reporter who raced from the crowded courtroom to spread the news following the verdict, the judge had said:

"'Stand up, yah voracious man eating son if a bitch, stand up!' Thin, p'intin' his

Granite blocks from the quarry at Aberdeen, eight miles west of Gunnison, were used to construct the State Capital building in Denver. Roy C. Dunbar is the teamster-mule skinner. Seated are Fred "Fritz" Zugelder, Karl Zugelder, Dick Bryan and his son. Horse teams are "Phoebe and Queen" in the lead, "George and Dago" on swing, and "Kid and Bean" on wheel.

Ute Indian reservation and beyond the Territory of Colorado. Packer was sentenced to 40 years in prison. With a crusade by the muckraking Denver Post and its sob sister (gossip) Polly Pry, he was pardoned in 1901 on the condition that he remain in Colorado the rest of his life. He died in Littleton in 1907.

The Packer saga continued in the early 1990's as an expedition of forensic archeologists from the University of Arizona located the gravesite and unearthed bones to try to verify the slaughter. They concluded the slaughter had happened, and from the condition of the bones the Packer tale was true.

Aberdeen

Six miles southwest of Gunnison a large deposit of high quality granite was found on south Beaver Creek and became known as the Aberdeen quarry. The granite was highly valued and was chosen as the material to build the state capital building in Denver in 1889.

The Rio Grande extended a six-mile branch line to the quarry in July of that year. The quarry operated from August 1889 to April 1892 and five to twenty-five cars were shipped out daily. With little demand for granite following the completion of the State Capital, the quarry shut down and the tracks were pulled in 1904.

The mineral rich West Elk Loop area also contributed marble for the floors of the state capital from the J. C. Osgood quarry along Yule Creek at Marble, helping make sure the building was constructed of Colorado - only materials, including the gold covered dome.

tremblin' finger at Packer, so ragin' mad he was, 'They was sivin Dimmycrats in Hinsdale County, and ye et five iv thim, God damn ye. I sintins ye t'be hanged be the neck ontil ye're dead, dead, dead, as a warnin' ag'in reducin' the Dimmycratic popyalashun iv th' state.'"

The actual pronouncement by the judge, reputed to be an educated Southerner, was somewhat more studied, referring to Packer's crime as "...a murder revolting in all its details..." in the San Juan Mountains, where "At that time the hand of man had not marred the beauties of nature, the picture was fresh from the hand of the Great Artist who created it.

"Whether your murderous hand was guided by the misty light of the moon, or the flickering blaze of the campfire, you can only tell," said the judge. "No eye saw the bloody deed performed; no ear save your own caught the groans of your dying victims. You then and there robbed the living of life, and then robbed the dead of the reward of honest toil which they had accumulated... I know you have drunk the cup of bitterness to its very dregs..."

Packer was moved to Gunnison for safe keeping, but before the hangman had his day an appeal on a technicality opened a new trial in Gunnison in 1886. Packer was again found guilty, but the death sentence was overturned because the murders had taken place on what, at the time, was the

Mining and mules were the order of the day in the high country.

The Gunnison Gold Belt

Twelve miles south of Gunnison, and slightly west, in a barren expanse of sage hills was the town of Vulcan, the mainstay of the Gunnison Gold Belt. Mining had taken place in Vulcan as early as 1892 with the Midland and Continental Mines. In 1894, however, the biggest strike, a vein of quartz 22 feet wide, was discovered. Vulcan boomed.

The progress of the new gold camp was hampered, however, as the three mines, the Vulcan, Mammoth Chimney, and Good Hope, were all located on the same vein and instigated considerable legal activity to settle claims of ownership.

By August 1895 a population of 500 lived mostly in tents. But the strikes proved rich and the town grew. Streets were laid out and buildings constructed. In October 1895 the Vulcan mine was purchased for $100,000 by a syndicate headed by David Moffat, legendary Colorado banker, gold baron, and railroad builder. Horse teams were soon hauling ore to the Rio Grande railhead at Iola.

Labor unrest hit Vulcan in 1899 when aggravated union miners from Baldwin invaded the town and cut the phone lines, captured the post office and confiscated all arms. Seventeen non-union miners were marched through snow to Iola and shipped out. Later, 20 union miners were charged with disturbance and larceny. They were all acquitted.

Litigation hampered the operation of mines in Vulcan, and in 1900 Chinese miners came to town, indicating a downturn in fortunes. Mining was intermittent through 1906, when a large sulfur mining operation was started in the sulfur-rich area. By 1907, over 10,000 tons of sulfur were shipped from Vulcan. A sulfur refinery was built in 1909, processing ten tons per day. A disastrous fire struck Vulcan in 1910 when lightning struck a shaft, igniting 20 tons of sulfur, which burned all surface buildings. The sulfur operation was never rebuilt.

Vulcan rose a third time from its ashes when large copper deposits were discovered and a 40-ton smelter was built in 1916. Thirty men were employed through World War I after which the venture failed. Vulcan never came back and today is visible only by its mining dumps, a few derelict buildings and the marks of old roads in the sagebrush.

POINTS OF INTEREST

Crawford to Gunnison, 66 miles

• Crawford Reservoir, part of federal Smith Fork project, camping and recreation area and a Colorado State Park. Mile 1

• Turnoff to Black Canyon National Monument south rim. Eleven miles to spectacular views. Access is paved part way.

• Needle Rock view, volcanic cone, mile 2

• Maher, once a ranchland community, mile 4

• Gould Reservoir, irrigation for Fruitland Mesa, mile 7

• Crystal Creek trail to Black Canyon, mile 10

• Black Mesa, mile 20

• Hermit's View, mile 23, spectacular views of Black Canyon

• Pioneer Point trailhead, mile 35, access to Black Canyon and Curecanti Needle.

• Blue Mesa Dam, mile 38, Blue Mesa Reservoir, marina, access to upper end of Black Canyon. Intersection of US 50.

• Sapinero, mile 40.

• East on US 50 along Blue Mesa Reservoir for 20 miles. Elk Creek marina, visitor's center mile 50. Headquarters for the Curecanti National Recreation Area.

• Road to Lake City and the San Juan country, mile 59.

The Gunnison Country

Captain John Gunnison.

Gunnison

Long before the railroads and long before US Highway 50, Cochetopa Pass, "the pass of the buffalo" as the Ute Indians called it, was the only route into the Gunnison country. A long established trail, Cochetopa Pass led into the Gunnison Valley from the San Luis Valley to the southeast. This was the route by which the Utes traveled across the Continental Divide, as did the mountain men, fur trappers, explorers and pioneers.

One of the first explorers drawn to this low lying gap was the mountain man Antoine Robidoux. Born near St. Louis in 1794, Robidoux served a brief stint in the War of 1812 and was later introduced to the fur business by his friend August Choteau. Robidoux came west to Santa Fe in 1824, married a Mexican girl in order to obtain Mexican citizenship, and, therefore, gain a trapping and trading license.

Robidoux, who became president of the Santa Fe town council in 1830, had forged a trail from Taos to Fort Robidoux, which he built in 1828, on the Gunnison River near present day Delta, at the mouth of the Uncompahgre Valley. The fort provisioned mountain men from the Gunnison country and those traveling the north-south trail from New Mexico to the Green River, which was rich in beaver.

On a trip through the San Luis Valley in the 1830s, Robidoux crossed Cochetopa Pass from the San Luis Valley and passed through the Gunnison Valley heading west. At first the route seemed straightforward and easy, until Robidoux reached the mouth of the Black Canyon. Here, like the many who followed him, he veered south and struggled through the rugged hills approaching Cerro Summit.

The first official exploration of the Gunnison country occurred 20 years later and was led by Captain John Gunnison, for whom the city of Gunnison is named. Gunnison was an officer of the Army Topographical Engineers. He was chosen

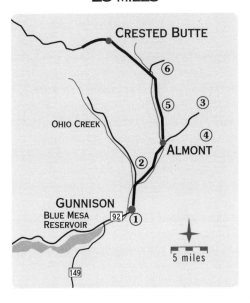

GUNNISON TO CRESTED BUTTE
28 MILES

1. Gunnison Visitor's Center at park Gunnison Musem, accross US 50 Western State College, east of Visitor's Center
2. Ohio Creek Road, mile 4 on Hwy 135 North
3. Taylor Park access, mile 9
4. Tincup
5. Roaring Judy Fish Hatchery, mile 14
6. Cement Creek, mile 22

by Secretary of War Jefferson Davis in 1853 to survey the unknown West for a transcontinental railroad route between the 38th and 39th parallels.

At age 41 Captain Gunnison was an experienced explorer, having spent 11 years exploring and mapping in the Utah wilderness. An adventurer, Gunnison was not one to shy away from risk. In the Laramie Valley of Wyoming, while running down buffalo and shooting them from horseback, Gunnison accidentally shot his own horse in the head, killing it and almost killing himself when the horse fell dead.

Gunnison's 1853 survey team consisted of 32 mounted riflemen, sixteen six-mule wagons, an instrument carriage pulled by four mules, and a four-mule ambulance. With him was a scientific staff, a botanist, artist and astronomer, who would research and render drawings of the region.

The party left Fort Leavenworth, Kansas on June 15, and set out across the prairies. The first mountains they encountered at La Veta Pass required them to drag and rope the wagons for ten grueling days before entering the San Luis Valley. With mountain man Antoine Leroux as guide they crossed 10,032-foot Cochetopa Pass on September 2. The gentle, comparatively low pass was seen as a promising route for a railroad.

The Gunnison Valley, a mile wide and abundant with fish and game, seemed like a paradise to the expedition members. They passed easily through the valley where the city of Gunnison lies today. They encountered their first major obstacle 15 miles west at the canyon of the Lake Fork of the Gunnison. As they struggled to

Gunnison in the 1880s, the west side of Main Street, looking north toward snow-covered Carbon Peak and Whetstone Mountain.

cross the Lake Fork, scouts brought daunting news of an even greater gorge beyond. Captain Gunnison and several men hiked into the entrance of the Black Canyon, near today's Blue Mesa Dam, and realized, after ten miles of sheer walls and a snarling river that it was impassable.

Gunnison swung south to avoid the canyon and hit the rugged terrain leading to Cerro Summit. His men hacked and cursed their way through this hilly, scrubby land, and at one point had to carry their wagons and supplies. Gunnison reasoned that Cochetopa Pass and the Gunnison valley would be impractical and cost prohibitive as a railroad route.

A month later, while exploring near Lake Sevier in Utah, Gunnison and a party of 11 men split off from the main group. They encountered hostile Paiute Indians who were vengeful from the killing of one of their band by a previous party of emigrants. In retaliation the Paiutes attacked the Gunnison party while they ate breakfast in camp. A volley of rifle shots and arrows killed all but four who escaped. Captain Gunnison was riddled with 14 arrows. The bodies of the victims were found the next day horribly mutilated - their arms cut off at the elbows and their entrails exposed. Their limbs had been chewed by wolves.

Lieutenant Edward Beale and John C. Fremont, "Pathmaker of the West," crossed through the Gunnison country with separate expeditions that same year. Both experienced the same difficulties to the west of the Gunnison Valley, first

A burro pack train forms in Gunnison in the 1880s to carry provisions to outlying mining camps.

Sylvester Richardson, the father of Gunnison.

hampered by the Lake Fork canyon, then blocked by the Black Canyon, and finally burdened with Cerro Summit, which later became known as "Son-of-a-Bitch" hill.

A group of Denver cattlemen tried the Gunnison country in 1862, but the severity of the winter chased them out. According to an account, "they were glad to escape with their lives eastward on snowshoes, leaving their cattle numbering several hundred to the mercy of the elements. Of the latter, all perished except a single mule, which they found alive on their return the following spring."

Deemed an unsuitable route for a rail-road, plagued by severe winter weather, and recognized as Ute territory, development of the Gunnison country was shelved for a decade. Though placer mining was pursued in remote areas of the Elk Mountains, the Gunnison country remained a void on the maps.

One placer mining camp, Minersville, at Washington Gulch north of Crested Butte, supported 1,000 daring miners who scoured the hills and extracted $1 million worth of gold in 1861. Once the ore played out, however, the Elks were again deserted. A Ute massacre of 12 miners in Washington Gulch in 1862 sent a harsh warning that this was still forbidden land.

It wasn't until Ferdinand Hayden explored the Gunnison country in 1873 that the region became known. Photographer William H. Jackson accompanied Hayden and recorded the stunning topography on glass plates. Hayden, a doctor turned geologist, loved the Elk Mountains, and so did his men. They covered the Elk Range with a passion, leaving reluctantly when their work was completed. Hayden's "Rover Boys" left the Gunnison country in 1875, having produced maps, and photographs, and having identified potential mineral orebodies.

With the Utes removed permanently from Colorado in 1881, the Gunnison country was opened to settlement on a scale never before imagined. Gold, silver and coal brought miners from far and wide. The promise of a boom town fueled

A Gunnison man astride an ox drags a barrel of water on a sled through downtown Gunnison. This was part of the water system!

the growth of Gunnison City with staggering speed. A Denver newspaper reported the promise of the new land in the summer of 1880:

"'To the Gunnison' is the all absorbing subject of thought and talk in Denver as well as on the remotest borders of the country, just now, and one is almost inclined to believe that if only one half of those go who build castles in the air about the Gunnison ... there will be such a rush that the country cannot hold them. At all events the Gunnison excitement is the prevailing epidemic at present..."

The founding father of Gunnison was Sylvester Richardson, a sturdy explorer and visionary who explored the Gunnison country on foot in 1873, walking 600 miles through the rugged Elk Mountains. He envisioned a great city, perhaps even the capital of Colorado, in the wide, fertile valley of the Gunnison. All roads would lead to Gunnison, said Richardson, who in 1874 created a joint stock company to found and build the city of his dreams.

Despite a dispute which split the city into two companies, Richardson held to his vision and founded Gunnison in 1874. That winter only 20 people stayed. The following spring interest waned because gold strikes in the San Juan Mountains were still the main "excitement." By 1878, however, mining activity in the Gunnison country had increased, and by 1879 Gunnison was the talk of the West.

Soon prospectors, freighters, and stage companies came to Gunnison over a dozen mountain passes, some worthy only of the sure footed burro, others wagon ready. The great road builder, Otto Mears, drove a road over Marshall Pass, near present day Monarch Pass, and extended it to Lake City and into the San Juans.

Despite the harsh winter weather, the rugged condition of the roads, and the great distance from the closest railhead, the allure of gold and riches created a boom that engulfed Gunnison in a steady flow of people and goods.

As one account describes, "The long row of tents and the bright campfires stretching along the east bank of the Gunnison made a spectacular panorama during the summer nights of 1880, and the continuous braying of hundreds of burros disturbed the peace of the sleep inclined all through the night." Behind the miner came merchants, speculators, newspaper editors, saloon keepers, restaurants, hotels, churches and two railroads, the Denver & Rio Grande and the Denver South Park. Gunnison had all the trappings of a burgeoning city.

Booms are often followed by busts, however, and Gunnison busted only a decade after Richardson had laid the groundwork for his great Gunnison City. His bold expectations had proved greater than reality. The surrounding mines failed to produce at the level of frenzy they had spurred.

As with most boosterism, hyperbole painted a brighter picture than the land could provide. The falling price of silver, even before the crash of 1893, closed many mines. Others were under-capitalized. Still, optimism ran high and other ventures were brought to Gunnison.

A major smelter was built on Tomichi Creek in 1886 to make Gunnison a center for reduction of ore. It closed in 1888 because of financial problems and a lack of ore. There was a major lumberyard in Gunnison, which also failed due to the slowdown. Thousands of tons of ice were shipped out each winter, filling 25 railroad cars a day, and four major brickyards were producing 400,000 bricks a week. But Gunnison had slipped into a depression. By the 1890s, most large businesses had failed or closed shop.

In the aftermath of the "excitement" coal deposits were developed in the Ohio Creek Valley and Crested Butte. There were several gold strikes south of Gunnison, and the cattle industry grew into a slow but steady economic force. Coal, gold and cattle became powerful influences that stabilized Gunnison into a modest community through the early 20th century.

Western State College was opened in 1911 as a Colorado State Normal School. It later became an accredited college, attract-

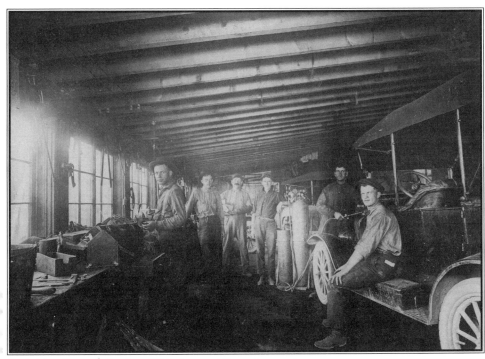

The Rainbow Garage in Gunnison, Will Hartman and George Aspey partners.

Alonzo Hartman and family at his palatial Gunnison home.

ing up to 3,000 students by the late 1960s. Today, tourism and recreation in the surrounding Gunnison National Forest account for a substantial portion of local revenues. Climate still remains a factor in the city's future, with Gunnison often recognized for the low temperature of the nation.

The Gunnison country, despite its early promise and the incredible boom years of the 1870s and 80s, was humbled by economic forces beyond its control, and by the finite mineral content of its mountains and river valleys. The boom turned to bust, and Gunnison was forced to accept a more humble, perhaps more suitable role, dwarfed as it is among the grandeur of the central Rocky Mountains.

Alonzo Hartman, Gunnison Cattle King

In 1875 the Ute Indians were moved west to the Uncompahgre Valley near present day Montrose. A young cattleman, Alonzo Hartman, of Iowa, followed them. Hartman had been hired in 1872 to manage cattle to feed the Utes at the Los Pinos Agency near Cochetopa Pass under a contract with the federal government.

"I rode a government mule from Los Pinos Agency to the government cow camp on the Gunnison River," wrote Hartman. "It snowed all day and we were soaking wet when we arrived in camp, but Jim Kelly soon had a good blaze in the fireplace and some hot coffee. Kelly and I spent the winter there without seeing anyone for over three months. We had 2,000 head of sheep and 3,000 head of cattle to take care of and the snow was getting deep, but we never lost a single one. We were busy boys riding every day and changing the cattle from place to place to keep them on the best feed we could find."

Hartman settled in the Gunnison Valley at the junction of the Gunnison River and Tomichi Creek where he later built his expansive ranch, "Dos Rios"(*Two Rivers*). Hartman was appointed postmaster of Gunnison in 1876. He and Kelly, still partners, opened a store in a small log cabin.

Hartman was postmaster for nine years, during which time he was often able to deliver the Gunnison mail in his vest pocket. By 1905 Hartman had parlayed his 160-acre ranch into 2,000 acres with 2,000 head of cattle. He left Gunnison in 1926 for California, where he died in 1940 at age 89. Hartman's Dos Rios "mansion" stands today as a private home.

A Tale of Two Railroads

First there were burros, then wagons, then stage lines. Transportation was the big key to opening the west. But the real mark of a thriving city was her railroads, and at its prime, Gunnison had two, the Denver & Rio Grande and the Denver South Park & Pacific. These narrow gauge lines pushed into the Gunnison country to tap its rich commerce of freight and ore in the early 1880s.

Both railroads were forced to contend with high mountain passes as they approached from the eastern slope in the Arkansas Valley. Cochetopa Pass was the most easily accessible route but it was farthest from both rail lines. Thus, other, more daunting routes were chosen, Marshall Pass and the Alpine Tunnel.

Both rail lines were driven by men of considerable force. William Jackson Palmer ran the Rio Grande. John Evans, a Colorado governor, and eastern financier Jay Gould, were among the South Park owners.

In the late 1870s General Palmer of the Rio Grande and Governor Evans of the South Park had a joint operating agreement. The South Park could use Rio Grande rails between Buena Vista and Leadville, while the Rio Grande would be permitted to use South Park rails into the Gunnison country. When Gould, the chief executive of the Union Pacific, bought the South Park line in 1880, however, the agreement was scrapped and the two railroads plunged into spirited competition. The South Park built its own rails to Leadville and the race was on to enter the Gunnison country.

The Rio Grande plowed its way over snowy Marshall Pass in a battle with the Denver & South Park to reach Gunnison. The Rio Grande arrived in August 1881, over a year before the troubled South Park.

The railroads had to make certain that a major capital outlay for the costly lines into Gunnison was justified. They could not rely on hyperbole from boosters to make such a decision, and there was plenty of bluster to encourage them. Both railroad companies knew the Gunnison country had silver and gold, but it was the region's vast coal reserves that made the grandiose plans to cross the Divide feasible. Not only would the coal of the Ohio Valley and the Crested Butte area fuel the railroads' steam engines, it would furnish coke and fuel for steel mills. And since the Divide had to be crossed if either railroad hoped to reach Salt Lake City, and later, California, it might as well be here and now.

Rio Grande crews began grading the four percent grade in November 1880 from Poncha Junction toward Marshall Pass. A cold snap that plunged temperatures to 23 below in Salida and colder still on the high grade, forced crews to quit in droves. Construction crawled that winter.

Through the next spring, however, the crews pushed hard, and the first passenger train arrived at the top of 10,856-foot Marshall Pass in June 1881. The Rio Grande thought it would have to tunnel beneath the top of the pass, but instead elected to blast a notch

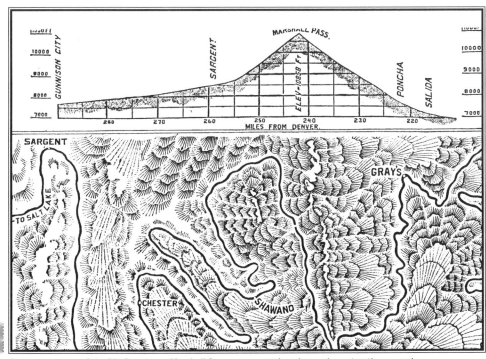

The tortous route of the Rio Grand over Marshall Pass was an engineering and construction marvel.

through rock and cover its tracks with a long, curving snowshed.

One of the engineering feats of the Rio Grande was a series of horseshoe curves that allowed the line to hold to its four percent grade. The track snaked back and forth in serpentine fashion through a series of sheltering snow sheds. On the west side of Marshall Pass the track meandered for 16 miles to drop 1,444 feet to a station called Chester.

Marshall Pass was named for Lieutenant William Marshall, who was part of the Wheeler Survey of 1873. Marshall was plagued by a toothache on the expedition and made a fast return to Denver, discovering the pass that now bears his name It was the quickest route to a dentist! Palmer had bought the old Marshall Pass toll road, opened by Otto Mears in the 1870s, for $13,000. He employed 1,100 men and 150 teams to grade and lay track.

The Rio Grande was the first railroad to reach Gunnison, arriving in August 1881. The grade over Marshall Pass had required the construction of 30 snowsheds to shield the tracks from the heavy snows and high winds at the Continental Divide. With around-the-clock labor and a dedicated work force driven by intense pride, the train rolled into Gunnison on a Sunday evening and was greeted by an exuberant throng.

"Sidewalks were almost a solid mass of moving humanity, while the hotels, restaurants, saloons, gambling houses, confectionery establishments, the varieties, etc., were as lively as a sugar cast in fly time."

The Denver South Park was plagued with greater difficulties. The railroad went up Chalk Creek from the Arkansas Valley and bored a 2,500-foot tunnel beneath the Divide. Built under impossible working conditions at 11,523 feet, the Alpine Tunnel required 500,000 board feet of California redwood timber.

Chosen for its flame retardant and rot resistant qualities, the redwood cost a fortune, not only to buy but to ship from California. Long snow sheds were constructed on either side of the tunnel. The railroad builders were then challenged to build a shelf for the train on its western descent past a vertical rock face called the "Palisades". A massive stone wall was made from hand hewn stone. It was assembled without mortar and stands today - 452 feet long, 33 feet high and two feet thick - as a memorial to the road graders and stone masons.

In September 1882, 13 months after the Rio Grande had steamed into Gunnison, the South Park made its entrance, and a town-wide beer bust was held to celebrate Gunnison's second railroad.

"The town was wide open that night," described a celebrant. "Hundreds of boxes were piled up in the middle of New York Avenue, near the railroad, and set afire. On either side of the roaring flames were long rows of beer kegs, all inviting the thirsty..."

The South Park ventured toward Mt.

Carbon and the coal mines of the Ohio Valley. Optimistically, the South Park forged further ahead in 1881 and built a grade from Baldwin toward Ohio Pass and the booming camps of Irwin and Ruby. Plans to continue the grade over Kebler Pass, as the next step on its transcontinental route, were halted far short of completion. A section of the grade known as the "Chinese Wall," a rock retaining wall built by coolie labor near Ohio Pass and visible from the 4-wheel-drive road, was named a Gunnison County Historic Landmark in 1997.

The Rio Grande completed its "Scenic Line of the World" route west through the Black Canyon in 1881, and built a major extension north to Crested Butte. On November 21, 1881 the first Rio Grande train entered Crested Butte.

"With a rapidity that is astonishing even to those accustomed to see it, the track was extended to the coal chutes at the west end of the town, and the first load of Crested Butte coal was put upon the cars," reported the Crested Butte *Republican*. The Rio Grande then pushed north of Crested Butte up the Slate River to the Smith Hill mine and west along Coal Creek beyond the summit of Kebler Pass to the coal mine at Floresta.

Despite this burst of rail activity, the economy of the region could not sustain one railroad, let alone two. The boom turned to bust and the railroads felt the effects by the early 1900s. When coal production declined and livestock, plus the "bedsprings and cornflakes" traffic, was transported by trucks on improved highways, freight dropped off dramatically. By 1910 a cave-in at the Alpine

Before the rails, it was strings of "jacks" that served as the freight carriers all over the steep mountain terrain, serving remote mines and mining districts, and the communities they engendered.

Tunnel terminated the South Park's route to the Gunnison country. Its tracks from Gunnison to the coal mining town of Baldwin in the Ohio Valley were inherited by the Rio Grande.

With a dramatic reduction of freight and a relocation of its main, transcontinental line through the Moffat Tunnel, the Rio Grande dropped to about one run a month by the 1940s. The Rio Grande applied to abandon its tracks west of Gunnison in 1948.

After the closing of the Big Mine in Crested Butte by CF&I in 1952, the route over Marshall Pass was discontinued. The last train ran through Gunnison and over Marshall Pass in 1954. The Rio Grande pulled up its tracks the following year. The Rio Grande gave the Marshall Pass grade to Saguache and Chaffee Counties for use as a road, and structures, ties and old rail cars were sold to anyone who made an offer. The railroad was gone and an exciting, dramatic era came to an end.

A sign at the La Veta Hotel enticed diners during its quiet years. The hotel only had to pay up rarely.

In the 1960s the dams of the Wayne Aspinall Storage Unit, Blue Mesa, Morrow Point and Crystal, submerged the Rio Grande's "Scenic Line of the World" beneath the impounded waters of the Gunnison. Marshall Pass and the approaches to the Alpine Tunnel have become 4-wheel drive roads.

A memorial to the railroads of the Gunnison country, once the hub of five narrow gauge lines, is a section of railroad bridge at Cimarron displaying little engine #278 attached to a short train. A display at Gunnison's Pioneer Museum contains a Rio Grande station, water tank, engine and short train, plus many railroad artifacts.

A Peacock Among Mud Hens

A first class hotel was just what Gunnison needed to give it an elevated sense of credibility and style. The La Veta, Spanish for "The Vein," fit the bill perfectly. The $212,000 four story hotel would be the pride of the West, according to its creator, Louden Mullin.

By 1883 the exterior was completed. Mullin, however, was nearly broke. He brought in a financial partner, Ben Lewis, a businessman from St. Louis, who staked him with $250,000 worth of Gunnison real estate. The hotel proceeded.

Some 2.5 million bricks were made in Gunnison for the hotel and a bank was incorporated in the building. There was a 40 x 50-foot billiard room and a luxurious bar featured the largest plate glass mirror in Colorado. A men's reading room, a huge dining room, and a rotunda lit by hammered glass skylights gave the hotel polish and elegance.

The grand stairway leading to the 107 sleeping rooms in upper floors was made from black walnut, and large balconies on the second and third floors opened to views of the sprawling city.

The hotel's opening was celebrated with a grand banquet. Guests from around the country came to Gunnison to experience the christening of a rare structure. After the banquet, a ball was held that rivaled the opulence of the capitals of Europe for its gaiety and luxury. Guests danced until dawn.

Ironically, the hotel's opening in 1883 marked the end of Gunnison's rich boom. Because of high operating costs and sparse occupancy, the hotel was forced to close during the winter of 1885-86, and for most winters thereafter. In 1889 the hotel was sold under a deed of trust and was passed around to many different owners.

In 1912 manager Joseph Howland advertised free meals on any day that the sun didn't shine in Gunnison. The hotel was forced to pay only 20 times in 40 years, a fact mentioned in Ripley's *Believe It or Not*.

In 1943 the hotel sold at auction to a lone bidder, J. H. Saunders, for $8,350. After its next sale, the building was leveled to the first floor for salvage. It served as low-rent apartments and cheap commercial space until recently, when its last remnants were removed.

The Gunnison Uranium Boom

Until 1995, on the south side of Gunnison, a large repository of uranium mill tailings was the only remnant of a uranium boom that hit Gunnison from 1955 to 1962. During that time, the Gunnison Mining Company of Vance and Garth Thornburgh employed 220 workers and paid out $70,000 per month in wages. Just as suddenly as it came in answer to a national need, the government–controlled price of uranium was reduced, the ore started to play out and the boom ended.

The radioactive tailings were trucked six miles east of Gunnison and impounded on BLM land adjacent to the county landfill.

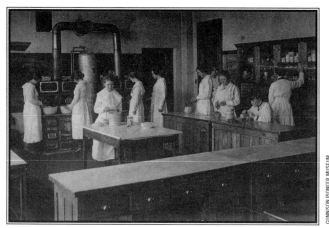

Home Economics classes were held in the basement of Taylor Hall during the old days of the Normal School.

Western State College opened as a normal school in 1911. Today, Taylor Hall is only one of many campus buildings at the four-year state college.

W Mountain and Western State College

Southeast of Gunnison stands a major landmark in the Gunnison Country - Tenderfoot Mountain, or, as it's better known, "W Mountain." The huge W is the symbol for Western State College of Colorado, which was built as a Colorado State Normal School in 1911. Gunnison Residents had petitioned for a college since the mid - 1880s, and the Normal School educated teachers and rural students during Gunnison's quiet years.

After World War II the GI Bill offered an incentive for ex-servicemen to seek higher education, and Western State College, as it had been re-named, attracted a growing student body. By 1947, Western State College boasted an enrollment of 600.

The ensuing "Baby Boom" further boosted WSC's enrollment to 1,000 in 1955, 2,000 in 1965, and 3,000 by the late 1960s.

The college contributes substantially to the local economy and offers Gunnison an intellectual and cultural center.

The W on "W Mountain" is whitewashed by college students in an annual fall ceremony. Until a decade ago, it was the largest single letter in the world. It is now the largest in the Western Hemisphere - 420 feet long and 320 feet wide. It's legs are 16 feet wide, and it covers 25,560 square feet.

Pioneer Museum

In 1964, with the purpose of preserving its pioneer history, the Gunnison County Pioneer and Historical Society began acquiring collections. Today they are extensive and artfully displayed on landscaped grounds on the east end of town.

The museum is comprised of eight buildings and includes an authentic railroad depot, narrow gauge train, water tank, a turn-of-the-century farmhouse filled with artifacts, and a schoolhouse complete with desks, chalk boards and photographs. Also on display are Alonzo Hartman's original 1876 log post office building, antique cars and wagons, ranching machinery and a dairy barn.

Information and exhibits are located in the outlying buildings and in the interpretive center which features an impressive collection of arrowheads and spear points.

The museum is open Memorial Day through Labor Day, Monday through Saturday, from 9 a.m. to 5 p.m. Tours are given by volunteers. Admission is $4 for adults and $1 for children, ages 6-12.

The Chamber of Commerce provides a walking tour map and historic descriptions of key buildings free of charge at the Chamber Visitor Information Center on E. Tomichi Avenue, one block west of the Pioneer Museum.

Sheep, like this herd on Crested Butte's Elk Avenue, incited Gunnison Country cattlemen to violently expel them from the open range.

Sheep Wars in the Gunnison Country

By the early 1890s cattle ranching was a major industry in the wide open Gunnison country. The Gunnison Stock Growers Association was formed in 1894 to protect the interests of cattlemen by thwarting rustlers and quarantining diseased cattle. A covert agenda, however, was to insure that sheep did not invade the open range and compete with cattle for precious grazing lands that had come to be viewed as the property of ranchers.

The first president of the Association was Alonzo Hartman, Gunnison's first and foremost rancher, who agreed with his contemporaries that sheep ought to be kept off the range. A number of stigmas weighed in the favor of the cattlemen.

Sheep, they charged, grazed down to the ground and decimated the native grasses, causing erosion. Sheep also left an odor on the ground that repelled cattle, they claimed. There was also a racial element to the anti-sheep campaign. Cattlemen were Anglo, while sheep herders were often Mexican or Basque.

The Association went so far as to ban from membership anybody who raised sheep in any number. This brought about a debate about the banning of two members for raising a few sheep for domestic purposes. At a lively meeting in 1902 the debate culminated when Hartman warned that "five could grow into 500." At that point, someone asked Hartman if

he didn't, in fact, eat mutton. The embarrassed rancher admitted, to the laughter of his peers: "Yes, but I am ashamed of it." The Association compromised by allowing members to raise sheep, but only for personal use and only if kept in pens.

Still, when sheep herders entered the Gunnison country, they were met with violent aggression. In June 1901, one of the worst slaughters in western Colorado history occurred near Iola, just west of Gunnison, when a sheep herder brought 10,000 head of sheep into Gunnison cattle country. That night, two sheep herders were confronted by a band of masked men who tied up one and ordered the other to leave the country. The "Night Riders" then proceeded to systematically slaughter 1,000 sheep and 1,300 lambs.

When the Gunnison National Forest was created in 1905, over a million acres were withdrawn from settlement. This effectively closed much of the free range Gunnison cattlemen had been using by placing it in federal control. The outcry was strong from cattle interests that the withdrawal of land would destroy the cattle industry in Gunnison.

Their protests were for naught, however, and the legislation stuck. Once they finally accepted the Forest Service and worked with it to conserve land, fight forest fires and regulate grazing, most cattlemen came to agree that the withdrawal was a long-term benefit that may have saved their ranges from overgrazing.

The cattlemen's proprietary view of public land in the Gunnison country was not quelled, however, and the cattle-sheep conflict boiled over again in 1918 when William Kruetzer, the first Forest

Ranger in the history of the Forest Service, came to the Gunnison National Forest. At issue was a sheep grazing permit Kruetzer had issued north of Crested Butte in the Oh-be-Joyful valley.

Kruetzer's life was threatened during a standoff on the sheep range when a group of cattleman, many of them apparently drunk, attempted to coerce the sheep operation out of the valley. One rancher shoved a cocked six-gun into Kruetzer's stomach and demanded that he promise to remove the sheep, to which the Ranger unwillingly agreed.

Several days later, three unknown riders tied up the two sheep herders in Oh-be-Joyful and forced many of their flock over the edge of a 20-foot cliff, killing 77 sheep and injuring 150.

A special investigator was called in and, though there were no convictions, the cattlemen of the Gunnison Country were put on notice that the government meant business and would prosecute to the limit of the law. This tempered the conflicts and the cattle-sheep wars drifted to an end.

Ohio Creek Valley

Five miles north of Gunnison, the Ohio Creek Valley veers west from the Gunnison Valley and State Highway 135, climbing 18 miles to 10,033-foot Ohio Pass. In the distance are Carbon Peak (12,079 feet), a conical mountain, and the long, undulating Anthracite Ridge, crowned by Ohio Peak (12,271 feet).

This wide, pastoral valley, set amid splendid mountain peaks, was first settled in the late 1870s as a ranching and coal

Stacking hay was part of life in the Ohio Creek Valley. Horse teams were used for swathing, raking and stacking.

mining region with good soil, plentiful irrigation water and huge bituminous coal deposits. The Valley skirts the eastern border of the West Elk Wilderness Area.

In antiquity the valley was the route of a Ute Indian trail that led from the Los Pinos Agency near Cochetopa Pass to the White River Agency near present day Meeker. The Ute Indians passed through the Gunnison Valley, climbed over Ohio Pass and Kebler Pass, then followed Anthracite Creek.

With the introduction of white settlers into the Gunnison Country, the Ohio Valley began to open as early as 1876 when a wagon road was built by the Crooke Brothers of Lake City, who had leased Sylvester Richardson's Mount Carbon Coal Mine. The Crooke Brothers mined and shipped coal to fuel their smelting plant in Lake City, and their toll road became the route for many pioneer ranchers.

Among them were Philip and Regis Vidal, from Paris, France, who homesteaded in 1875 and received the valley's most senior water rights. Regis, the eldest brother, died in 1901. He left behind $15,000 in debt, a wife and nine children, eight of whom were girls. To make ends meet, the girls put on overalls and worked the ranch to make their 750-acre spread prosper.

Ohio Creek rancher George Cornwall, originally from New York, was the first of the Gunnison country ranchers to plant a vegetable garden in spite of pessimism from his neighbors who thought the high

Not just the rich with their European-style zoos and gamekeepers, but folks like Bert Hildebrand had pet elk like this one near Gunnison.

altitude and cold temperatures would make such a venture hopeless.

After Cornwall's success, every ranching family began a garden. Cornwall founded the Gunnison County Agricultural Fair, which became a popular, county-wide event that preceded the every popular Cattlemen's Days. A large variety of produce was shown at the fair, plus livestock and mining exhibits. There were baking and jam contests, horse, trotting and burro races. Bands played and the farmers and ranchers celebrated the bounty of the land and the pioneer spirit that had brought them together.

Cornwall's neighbor in the Ohio Valley was a German immigrant named John Bohm. Frugal to a fault, Mrs. Bohm made use of everything, including heavy cotton flour sacks, from which she made clothing. Cornwall's son, Harry, visited the Bohms one day and was greeted at the door by Mrs. Bohm, who inspired the following description.

"She was wearing a blouse and a skirt made from flour sacks, and with an eye to artistic effect had made the garments in such a way that the stencil marks giving the names of the brands of flour in red letters about three inches high appeared symmetrically upon the garments. Mrs. Bohm was rather a plump woman. Across her bust was "Pride of the Family," and across her skirt "Rough and Ready" - these being the favorite brands of flour at that time."

Another episode with the Bohms found Harry Cornwall buying butter from his German neighbors. When he was led into the butter shed in the dead of winter, Harry noticed a large, wrapped bundle on the shelf above. Bohm answered Cornwall's inquiry with a matter-of-fact explanation that his wife's cousin had died, and they were keeping the body cool until proper burial after spring thaw. The body was on a shelf just above the butter. Cornwall later remarked that he took the butter, but didn't eat any until that lot was gone.

In the early 1880s Ohio Creek became a logging region with three saw mills operating for the building needs of booming Gunnison. Halls Saw Mill was located on Mill Creek, several miles west of the Ohio Creek Valley; the Clark & Stewart Mill manufactured planks further north, near Carbon Peak; and a mill operated by Jack Haverly, the multimillionaire minstrel, and C. S. Boutcher processed timber two and a half miles from King's Ranch, near the base of Ohio Pass.

Ohio Pass was the most direct conduit

to the mining camps of Irwin and Ruby, and supplies were hauled there as soon as the deep snows receded in the spring of 1880. Miners flocked to the region, and there was a string of them heading over the muddy pass road by June via Ohio Creek.

A temporary camp at the base of Ohio Pass was called Skinnerville for Jim Skinner, a mercantile owner. Freighters were hired at ten cents a pound to carry goods over the pass on their backs. Many made the trek on skis, starting in the early morning when the snow was crusted. *Elk Mountain Pilot* newspaper publisher John E. Phillips had his press, type, ink, paper and other materials carried to Ruby over the snow.

Baldwin and Castleton were built in the Ohio Valley coal region. Castleton was incorporated in 1882 as the focal point for the Mount Carbon coal mine, whose coal reserves were used for fuel by the Denver South Park Railroad. Castleton furnished the necessities of pioneer life: stores, saloon, billiard hall, restaurant, homes and a school. It also served as a freight center for the mining camps near Ruby Gulch.

When Ruby failed and the South Park Railroad halted its service, Castleton's fortunes declined and attention shifted to Baldwin.

A creamery and cheese factory were established in Castleton in 1887 and produced cheese and butter from the 1,500 to 1,800 pounds of milk delivered each day by Gunnison country dairymen. The high-quality cream and cheese were shipped across the West. A fire burned the creamery in 1892, ending the temporary rebirth of Castleton.

Mules strain to pull a coal cart in a coal mine. Mules were the only power source in the mines until the early 1900s, and the coal companies often valued them more than the miners.

Coal Mining and Baldwin

Baldwin became the population center for the Ohio Valley when the coal deposits of Mt. Carbon were fully exploited. Despite half a dozen futile ventures to drill for oil in the coal-rich Ohio Valley, it was coal that provided a steady energy industry.

The South Park Coal Company, owned by the South Park Railroad, opened a mine and built cabins in 1881, calling the new development Baldwin for the private secretary of the superintendent for the Colorado Division of the Union Pacific Railroad.

By 1882, the Castleton-Baldwin developments had encouraged seven other mines to open in the area, and the orders for coal shipments were so promising that the South Park Railroad built track up Carbon Creek with plans to cross Ohio Pass to Irwin. By the late 1880s, however, the plans failed and the track made it only several miles past Castleton.

Aside from its prominence as a coal mining center for the Gunnison country, Baldwin had the distinction of hosting the first football game in Gunnison County history. The match occurred in 1888 with Crested Butte. A referee from each town was chosen to supervise play. When the Crested Butte referee became too drunk to perform his duties, the Baldwin referee had to attempt the impossible task alone. The game was rough and tumble, and celebrants opened kegs to celebrate each touchdown.

Baseball was another popular pastime and Baldwin fielded a team to compete against Crested Butte, Jack's Cabin, Gunnison and, once, a Choctaw Indian team from Oklahoma. Prize fighting also came to town and occasionally inspired better brawls between spectators outside the ring than those in the ring. In 1938 a 700-foot toboggan run was built on a 35-degree slope to excite and thrill daring sledders.

When they weren't playing at sports or working the mines, Baldwin miners enjoyed polka dances as a regular distraction from their grueling work and ruthless exploitation by mine management.

Like many coal mining towns, Baldwin was not much to look at. Ramshackle buildings, dirt and mud streets, and a pall of coal dust in the air and on the ground caused one observer in 1903 to describe it as possessing "all the hideousness which belongs to those unhappy looking settlements".

Labor disputes cropped up regularly in Baldwin over safety issues concerning the Alpine mine, where poor ventilation and lax inspections contributed to the deaths of ten men from 1898 to 1946, with many more injured. Intimidation and violence

1887 – 1922

were often the result of clashes between miners and management.

In 1886 a fight broke out among the miners during a prize fight, and Hugh McCabe killed Baldwin miner Luke Curran by slashing his stomach with a knife. McCabe, while awaiting trial in Gunnison, killed himself by slashing his wrists with a straight razor.

It was later discovered that McCabe was really Tom Hurley, a member of the notorious Molly McGuires wanted by Pinkerton detectives for murder and inciting violence against replacements for striking miners in Pennsylvania.

From 1883 to 1892, the miners of Baldwin produced 26,000 tons of coal a year. Most went to the South Park Railroad; the rest was shipped to precious metal smelters in Golden and Leadville. The Alpine Mine was the richest of the

Baldwin-area mines. Production there peaked in 1904 when 121 men mined 111,283 tons.

Ten strikes occurred in the Baldwin mines between 1886 and 1900, but the union was too weak to be effective. When the miners protested dangerous working conditions they either quit or were fired. When non-union "Negro" miners were hired in 1900, striking miners burned the South Park Railroad tipple in protest. The South Park Railroad bridge crossing the Gunnison River was blown up that same year, supposedly by angry miners.

In 1904, heeding the complaints of Baldwin miners, the United Mine Workers of America sent an aide, W. W. Wardjohn, to the Gunnison country. Wardjohn never made it. He was intercepted in his rail car on his way over Marshall Pass and beaten by three anti-union men. Frightened off, he returned to Denver. It wasn't until 1928 that the United Mine Workers was able to organize labor at the Alpine mine.

Baldwin produced coal until March 31, 1946. The miners had planned a strike for April 1, so the Alpine Fuel Company closed the mine the day before the strike could be carried out. The company feared violence associated with the strike, and it also knew most of the best coal had already been exhausted.

The Alpine mine was never reopened, and Baldwin remains today as a ghost town of scattered buildings amid sagebrush. The grave of coal miner Joe "Peanuts" Berta is at the old townsite, honoring a long-time resident and "Man of the Mountains".

Almont

The resort village of Almont, ten miles north of Gunnison on Highway 135, lies at the junction of the East and Taylor Rivers, whose combined flow creates the Gunnison River. Almont was not a mining camp, but a crossroads for commerce and trade among Gunnison, Taylor Park, Crested Butte and the mining camps of the northern Elk Mountains.

Almont begins with the story of Sam Fisher, an Easterner with a degree in mining engineering from a prestigious university who came west in the 1860s, following the call of the mining camps. Fisher came into the Gunnison country with his new wife, mother, grandmother and brother. His first job was as a freighter between Gunnison and Gothic.

Enroute to Gothic, Fisher had to cross the Taylor River at present day Almont, where a rickety bridge required a toll. Fisher decided the toll business was more lucrative than freighting, and he applied for official permission from the Gunnison County Commissioners to build a road, bridge and tollgate at the river junction. He returned to the rickety bridge and informed the man then collecting tolls that he had the bridge permit. The man shrugged his shoulders and left the country.

Fisher improved the bridge and constructed several toll roads. He charged a dollar for a two-horse team, 50 cents for a horse and buggy, and 25 cents for a man on horseback. With the rush to the mining districts on the East and Taylor Rivers, Fisher became wealthy. By 1881 the Barlow and Sanderson Stage Line ran two stages a day through

In the early days, two-foot-long trout were plentiful in the streams and rivers of the Gunnison country. The Almont fish fry utilized hundreds of trout at the annual banquet.

Almont, and 500 travelers passed there each week.

Fisher's business was curtailed once the Rio Grande opened its branch line to Crested Butte in 1881, but his name was identified with the crossroads until that same year, when he changed the name to Almont, after the famous Hambletonian stallion "Almont." Fisher raised horses and purchased an offspring of the great horse and named him "Firmont."

In 1893, Fisher sold Almont to Vernon Davis, who turned the town into a resort boasting health-restoring waters, an excellent climate, and great fishing. The town had a post office, a railroad depot, and a thriving zinc mine, the Doctor Mine. A publicity publication from 1905 described Almont with poetic liberty: "The Taylor River comes dancing through the gorgeous canon to meet its sister, East River...and the two join hands together forever and form the mighty Gunnison."

In 1927, the first annual Almont fish fry was held, which became a popular tradition. In 1940 the July Fourth annu-

al event hosted 10,000 guests. Wendell Wilkie, a Republican presidential candidate, made a campaign stop in Almont and spoke from the railroad loading platform.

Wilkie's speech was covered by dozens of newspaper reporters, and the candidate mingled with the crowd as thousands partook of fried trout caught in local streams.

Today, Almont remains much as it was at the turn of the century-a collection of old cabins on the "dancing" waters of the Taylor and East Rivers, a popular summer resort community with great fishing at the crossroads of two spectacular river valleys.

The Almont Triangle

The Almont Triangle is a section of sagebrush covered hills with southern exposure and good forage that stretches between Almont and Jack's Cabin, and is bounded on the east by the Taylor River. In 1994 the Colorado Division of Wildlife and the U.S. Forest Service officially closed the Almont Triangle to human activity during the winter months when

The Sawatch Range is the high, rugged eastern border of Taylor Park. It was through passes in these high mountains that the first miners came to Tin Cup Gulch in 1860. Taylor Reservoir was created in 1937 by Taylor Dam and attracts thousands of boaters and fishermen every year. The impounded water is dedicated to a major irrigation project for the Uncompahgre Valley through the Gunnison Tunnel.

big game animals are stressed. The preserve is essential winter range for elk, deer and bighorn sheep, which have traditionally wintered there. The closure is effective December - March. The old Rio Grande railroad spur to Crested Butte is seen on the west side of the highway.

Taylor Park

East of Almont, 16 miles up the snaking Taylor Canyon, lies Taylor Park. "The Valley of the Gods," as the Utes referred to this thirty-mile-long, eight-mile-wide valley, was rich with fish and game, abounding in buffalo before the first prospectors of the 1860s ushered in the legions that followed in the booming 1870s.

Taylor Park is bordered to the east by the Sawatch Range, a part of the Continental Divide. Innumerable streams spill off into the Taylor Park drainage, eventually channeling into the Taylor River. At first accessible only by crossing high mountain passes, Taylor Park was forbidden ground to most settlers during early exploration.

Taylor Pass, at 11,900 feet, crosses the Elk Mountains north into the Roaring Fork Valley and the historic towns of Ashcroft and Aspen. Lake Pass, to the east, at 12,000 feet, was first used by the Utes to cross the Continental Divide from the Arkansas Valley near current day Twin Lakes. Lake Pass was used by Ferdinand Hayden and his Rover Boys during their exploration of the Gunnison country in 1873-75. Lake Pass would later fall out of favor due to its steep approaches and high elevation, but during the 1860s, it was the chief route into Taylor Park.

The first known white men to enter the valley were a group of "Forty-niners" from Georgia who had hired Cherokee Indians to guide them to the gold fields of California. They reportedly found some gold in Taylor Park, but not enough to keep them there. The park was officially discovered by Jim Taylor, a prospector who followed the wave of excitement to Colorado in the '59 gold rush. Despite the threat of Ute Indians, Taylor made his way over the Divide in 1860 from Granite, a small settlement in the Arkansas Valley.

Taylor tracked a band of Ute Indians as they headed west into their territory. They led him to the top of Lake Pass where Taylor saw the huge, enticing valley laid out below. He quickly returned to Granite and informed his three partners of his discovery. Even though it was October and winter was drawing near, the men horse packed over the pass and descended into the park. They camped near the site of present day Taylor reservoir, where their horses were run off by marauding bears.

While searching for the horses Taylor panned some gold out of Texas Creek and carried it to his partners in his tin drinking cup. The trail of the horses led the men further south to the site of what would become Tin Cup. Taylor discovered more gold on Willow Creek which he also carried to camp in his tin cup. As a result, he named the region Tin Cup Gulch.

The men were excited by what they had found in the remote and deserted valley, and they continued panning gold until late October when they realized the buffalo had fled the valley. Winter was on its way, so the men broke camp and raced back over Lake Pass just in time for the first blizzard of the winter. Frostbitten and exhausted, they lost their horses and barely made it to Granite.

By February the Taylor party was ready to embark with new supplies for Taylor Park. Two more partners were added to the expedition, and other miners had caught wind of the promising new region to the west. Taylor and party left Granite in February and attempted to lose another party of miners led by Fred Lottis, who followed them to discover the new land. Taylor and his party eventually reached Taylor Park. When they arrived, conditions were trying - ten below zero and six feet of snow on the ground.

The Lottis Party, which followed Taylor, lost its way in a blizzard and ended up in nearby Union Park, a name they gave in honor of the Civil War which had just broken out. The Lottis party found good camping and running water for the sluice boxes. They began placer mining before Taylor had enough water to begin his operation in Tin Cup Gulch.

Hundreds of miners followed these prospectors into Taylor and Union Parks that summer of 1861, panning every stream in the valley. There were no major

The Tin Cup Town Hall stands in good condition today after more than a century in the mountains.

strikes, but for the patient placer miner there was sufficient income. While Taylor and party left the park after the summer and went east to join the Confederate Army, Lottis stayed and made a comfortable living, sluicing $5,000-6,000 dollars every summer and spending winter months in Pueblo or Denver.

Following 20 years of mining in Union and Taylor Parks, Lottis sold his many mining claims in 1881 for $55,000. Lottis never gave up his prospecting zeal, however, and kept venturing into the backcountry. He froze to death enroute to one of his mining claims near Ohio City in February 1900 at the site where he and his party had been lost in the blizzard while tracking Taylor in the spring of 1861.

The big change for Taylor Park came in 1878 with the discovery of the Gold Cup mine south of Tin Cup. The ore assayed to be rich, and the rush was on. Two

towns sprang up - Virginia City, the scheme of miners from the Black Hills, and Hillerton, named for Edwin Hiller, a Denver banker.

Hillerton rode the crest of a wave that collapsed in 1880 as new excitements tantalized the fickle miners and all the commerce that went with them. Gothic had become the new word for boom town in the Elk Mountains. Virginia City and a new, nearby town of Abbeyville drew the remaining population. By 1900, not one building remained standing in Hillerton. They had all been moved to new prospects.

Tin Cup

By 1883, Abbeyville had gone the way of Hillerton as did a booming camp called Garfield. Virginia City, later named Tin Cup, became the town center for Taylor Park, a rip-roaring frontier mining town where the sixshooter became the dispenser of justice and the practice of law was a casual affair at best.

Only 120 hearty miners, their wives and children wintered over in Tin Cup in 1979-80, but the following summer thousands of miners flooded the region and scoured every mountain peak and river drainage for gold. Mines sprang up like gopher holes. Gold Cup, Drew, Tin Cup, Jimmy Mack, El Capitan, Anna Dedricka and Mayflower were among the names.

Wild and woolly, Tin Cup had a reputation as a brawling, violent outpost. The Gunnison *Daily News-Democrat* reported in 1882 that "The first comers were a hard crowd ... Feuds were common, and 'gun plays' were frequent occurrences. More than one man has bitten the dust

Hard rock mining took place all over the Gunnison country and caused the town of Tin Cup to flourish in the 1870s and early '80s. Gold and silver were plentiful in the region and fueled a major mining economy that centered in the rambunctious frontier town.

upon its streets, and the bullet holes in the sides of buildings still attest the bad marksmanship of the inhabitants. Had it been otherwise, the town would have been depopulated within the first six months of its existence."

Like many frontier mining towns, Tin Cup had an active and bawdy red light district. Among the female attractions were "Santa Fe Moll," whose name came from her previous career along the Santa Fe Trail; "Tin Can Laura," who made change for her clients from a tin can in her room; "Wishbone Mabel," whose bowed legs provided her nickname; "Sagebrush Annie," who was so-called because of the condition of her hair; and "Pass Out," a small, French girl who couldn't tolerate even one bottle of ale before passing out.

By 1882 Tin Cup was at its peak with upwards of 3,000 people living in the vicinity. The town had 20 saloons, five grocery stores, two butchers, four hotels and all the supporting businesses attached to a booming camp. The Tin Cup cemetery was divided into four sections, or knolls, one each for Catholics, Protestants, Jews and "Boot Hill" burials.

Tin Cup went into a decline in 1884, the victim of its own remoteness, harsh winters, deep snows, and failed smelters. Fires in 1906 and 1913 gutted most of the old downtown.

When the Silver Panic of 1893 hit, Tin Cup's population dropped to 200. A brief revival in 1904 brought 2,000 gold miners back to Tin Cup, but the gold was insufficient, and by 1911 the burst was over. A dredging operation in Willow Creek removed 20,000 ounces of gold between 1908 and 1912, but it lost money and was halted.

But Tin Cup fell into obscurity. The post office closed in 1918 and the town became a summer-only haven for fishermen and sportsmen. After World War II, it became a nearly-mythical town existing only on the radio as the brain child of Denver's legendary radio man Pete Smythe. He was "proprietor" of the general store and had an entire community operating, all from a studio in Denver.

Today, Tin Cup is a scattering of old buildings, most of which have been renovated as summer vacation cabins. Beautiful in its setting, what's left of the town stands as a reminder of the wild and fleeting glory days of the early mining booms.

Many other camps and hopeful towns sprang up in Taylor Park during the late 1800s and early 1900s. Over the years they all faded until their humble remains were mostly absorbed by the willows, aspens, lodgepole pines and spruce forests.

Taylor Reservoir

In 1935, work began on Taylor Dam, a project dating back to 1903. Western Slope Congressman Ed Taylor pushed for the project and Taylor Park Reservoir was officially approved in 1933.

Federal funding totaled $2,725,000, of which $2 million would be spent on the reservoir. Another $400,000 went to reline the Gunnison Tunnel, taking water from the Black Canyon to the lands around Montrose. Another $325,000 built canals in the Uncompahgre Valley, where the impounded water was designated to feed irrigation systems.

Rotary plows, like the one on this Rio Grande train, made it possible to cut through the deep snows of the East River Valley.

COLORADO HISTORICAL SOCIETY

The dam would provide water for the Western Slope, calming fears in Gunnison that the Taylor River and its many drainages would be tapped for the insatiable thirst of the metropolitan Eastern Slope.

Some 300 men worked to build the 168-foot-high dam from 1935-37. The dam would store 106,200 acre feet of water, supplementing irrigation for 75,000 acres on the Uncompahgre 75 miles away.

The dam was completed in November 1937 and today covers 2,030 acres of Taylor Park. The reservoir has become a major recreation attraction for boaters and fishermen. Some of the lowest winter temperatures in the Gunnison country are recorded at the dam, with dips in excess of 50 below zero.

Jack's Cabin

Five miles north of Almont, after Highway 135 climbs and winds through scrubby hills along the Almont Triangle, the East River Valley opens to a wide, flat plain six miles long and reaching up toward the Elk Mountains. This was the site of Howeville, or Jack's Cabin, as it came to be known for its originator, Jack Howe. There is a dirt road to the east, Jack's Cabin Cut-off, which connects to the Taylor River Road.

Howe homesteaded the land in 1875 and built a small cabin at this halfway point between Gunnison and Crested Butte that served as a stopover point for freighters and miners. According to *Crofutt's Gripsack Guide* of 1881, Jack Howe "was a prince of good fellows in his way. In the 'good old time,' a sojourn here for a few weeks to hunt and fish...with Jack as a companion and guide was one of the luxuries that went far to pay for the long and tedious journey over the mountain trails."

Located strategically at the intersection of the East River and a jack trail into Taylor Park, Jack's Cabin received considerable traffic. Jack and his partner Ben Sherwood built corrals and cabins, grew and stored hay, and opened a supply store.

By 1881, the settlement had a saloon, restaurant, post office and hotel, with another hotel being built to handle the overflow of miners and freighters filing up the valley toward elusive dreams and mining prospects.

When the Denver & Rio Grande Railroad pushed north to Crested Butte,

Avalanche was a constant scourge that took a steady toll on miners and railroad workers. This grim procession of rescuers is dragging the bodies of avalanche victims killed in 1884 at Woodstock, a small mining and railroad community south of Taylor Park. The town was destroyed, 13 died, and only 4 survived the deadly slide.

it built a siding to Jack's cabin that became a major railhead for shipping cattle and hay. Soon there was a school and cemetery. In 1905, a dairy opened and produced 25 pounds of Howeville Creamery butter each week.

Little is left today of the original Jack's Cabin except for the open plain and sweeping hills rising toward the divide of Spring Creek. Land development appears to be the future of the once thriving agricultural valley.

Roaring Judy Fish Hatchery

Begun as a private hatchery and mink farm, the Roaring Judy Fish Hatchery was bought by the State of Colorado in 1965. It is a prime facility because of pure spring water and wells, which generate a combined flow of 2000 gallons a minute.

Roaring Judy spawns Kokanee salmon, rainbow and Snake River native trout. The kokanee run naturally from Blue Mesa reservoir upstream to the hatchery, following the Gunnison and East Rivers. The spawning salmon are caught at the hatchery, where the eggs are taken from the females and fertilized. Once they have begun feeding, an average two million young kokanee are released each year from this essential spawning habitat into the East river to return to Blue Mesa.

Until whirling disease, caused by a European parasite, spread to all state hatcheries in the mid-1990s, these trout had been used to stock high mountain lakes and streams across southwestern Colorado. The whirling disease limited stocking of Roaring Judy's fish to Taylor and Blue Mesa reservoirs.

Cement Creek

Seven miles beyond Jack's Cabin, the Cement Creek Valley is a suburb of Crested Butte and Mt. Crested Butte. In the 1870s and '80s it was an access point to the Italian Mountain (13,378 ft.) mining camp above Taylor Park. First prospected by miners from Leadville, the camp had a thriving population of 150 in 1882 and was producing eight tons of galena, or lead ore, per day, valued at up to $70 a ton.

Mines in the Italian Mountain region included the Iron Chief, Marietta, Carbonate King, Star, Bull, Domingo, Black Prince, Black Princess, Silver Cloud and Monte Cristo. By 1895, the prospects had played out and the region fell into obscurity. Italian Mountain is the only known site in the western hemisphere where the gemstone, lapis lazuli, is mined.

Pioneer Ski Area

The Pioneer Ski Area on Cement Creek was opened during the winter of 1939-40 to cater to the skiing enthusiasm of the Gunnison country. The chairlift was fashioned from an old mining tram taken from the long abandoned Blistered Horn mine near the top of Cumberland Pass at the extreme southern end of Taylor Park. Chairs for the lift were hand-made, and the contraption was powered by a 450 horsepower engine, allowing skiers to ride to the top of the ridge and follow sweeping runs back to a lodge at the base area. The lift and ski area were later closed when the Forest Service declared the lift unsafe. The old ski runs are visible today as sweeping cuts in an otherwise solid forest of spruce.

Brush Creek

Five miles north of Cement Creek, across the valley from Whetstone Mountain (12,516 feet), Brush Creek borders the Skyland Golf Course and penetrates the remote mountains northeast toward 12,700-foot Pearl Pass. This rugged, rocky, 4-wheel-drive trail was one of the primary routes from Crested Butte to the booming mining camps of Ashcroft and Aspen during the 1870s, when it was frequented by jack trains and later by freight wagons.

The mail was first brought to Aspen over this demanding mountain pass, which today is relegated only to adventuresome four-wheelers, dirt bike riders and mountain bikers. Brush Creek and the Slate River have their confluence with the East River here.

The East River Valley has long been cattle country. Cowboys brave deep winter snows to care for their herds. Crested Butte Mountain is in the background with the northern Elk Mountains.

POINTS OF INTEREST

Gunnison to Crested Butte, 28 miles

• Gunnison has a visitor's center a block east of the main intersection on US 50. Across the highway is the extensive historical museum complex. Included there are railroad and pioneer days exhibits, including a narrow guage engine, water tank, and the original log cabin used as a post office.

• Western State College campus is off Highway 50 northeast of the Visitor Center.

• Heading north on Highway 135 brings you to the Ohio Creek turnoff, mile 4, to the west. Ohio Creek is the gateway to old mining towns such as Baldwin and Floresta, and Ohio Pass. This route is accessible with ordinary vehicles.

• Almont, mile 12, is the junction of the Taylor and East rivers, with the road to Taylor Park, Taylor Reservoir, and mining camps such as Tin Cup following the Taylor River to the east.

• Jack's Cabin is the intersection of another road east to Taylor Park.

• Roaring Judy fish hatchery, mile 21, is on the west.

• Cement Creek is access to old mining towns and the high country.

• Crested Butte, originally a coal mining community, is at mile 28.

Crested Butte and Kebler Pass

During its coal mining era, Crested Butte was a company town with company housing provided by CF&I. Scattered company houses remain today and Crested Butte Mountain defines the landscape to the east.

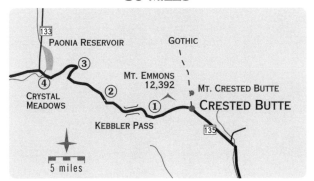

CRESTED BUTTE TO KEBLER PASS
30 MILES

Crested Butte

The great explorer Ferdinand Hayden, who wandered the Gunnison country in 1873-74 with his "Rover Boys," found his way to the head of the East River valley, where he climbed the dominant, triangular peak, Teocalli (13,220 feet). Scanning the incredible mountains of the Elk Range Hayden noticed two peaks he thought resembled the crests of helmets. They were Crested Butte and Gothic peaks. He named them "The Crested Buttes."

Placer miners had been in the area before Hayden, as early as the 1860s or before. These adventurers had lived perilously close to hostile Ute Indians who had massacred 12 miners in Washington

1. Lake Irwin, mile 5
2. Horse Ranch Park, mile 11
   trailhead
3. Dark Creek, Anthracite, mile 24
   Erikson Springs Campground
4. Crystal Meadows, mile 30
   Senic Byway information kiosk
   Return to Hwy 133 at Paonia Dam

Gulch, seven miles north of Crested Butte, and seven in Deadman's Gulch, 10 miles to the southeast.

Howard F. Smith, a partner in a smelter company in Leadville, was not intimidated by the Utes when he heard about huge coal deposits in Crested Butte. In 1878 he came into the East River by way of Taylor Park and acquired all the land near the confluence with Coal Creek and the Slate River. Smith found the coal he was after, but these vast coal deposits were not immediately developed.

Instead, Smith built a smelter and sawmill to profit from the surrounding hard rock mining camps, Irwin, Gothic, Pittsburgh, Elko, Schofield, Crystal, Ashcroft and Aspen. Crested Butte first figured prominently as a supply depot, lumber producer and smelting center, then later as a long-term coal producer. This made Crested Butte an atypical "boom town," where steady growth, as opposed to the wild, explosive growth of metal mining camps, gave it a feeling of permanence.

On July 3, 1880, Crested Butte was incorporated. The population was about 400. Smith, who served as the first mayor of Crested Butte in 1880, sold half his interest in the town and 1,000 acres of coal lands that year to William Jackson Palmer, owner of the Denver & Rio Grande railroad, as an enticement for the railroad magnate to finance an extension from Gunnison to Crested Butte. The Rio Grande arrived in 1881, assuring Crested Butte a dependable conduit for supplies and ore.

As Crested Butte drew income from neighboring silver camps, the town attract-

Crested Butte grew into a thriving community as a convenient center serving precious metal mining in the surrounding mountains as well as coal mining virtually beneath the community.

ed the interest of financiers like "silver czar" Horace Tabor who started the Crested Butte Bank in 1881. Newspapers were published to recount the news of the burgeoning town and boost its stature. The Crested Butte *Republican* was the first in a long line that included the Crested Butte *Gazette*, the *Elk Mountain Pilot*, and the *Weekly Citizen*.

Toll roads were built to Gunnison, Irwin, Gothic, and even to Aspen and Ashcroft. Hotels, like the Forest Queen, the Crested Butte House and Mrs. John Songer's boarding house were erected to provide amenities to visitors and discerning businessmen.

The Elk Mountain house, a huge building for its day, was built by the town

company in 1880-81 and served as the finest accommodation in town. The three-story hotel was 100x34 feet and took a year and a half to build. It had a large central stove that heated rooms through grates, with other stoves to provide heat in extremely cold weather. "Really, this Elk Mountain House surpasses all of the mountain hotels that I have stopped at," extolled geologist John Hallowell during a stay there in 1882.

The year of Hallowell's visit, Crested Butte had a population of 1,000. The town had five hotels, a dozen saloons, three livery stables, a dozen restaurants, five nearby sawmills, two doctors, countless lawyers and one church, the Union

The aftermath of a disastrous fire on January 9, 1893, with a view of the burned out town looking southeast from the corner of Elk Avenue and Second Street.

Congregational, which is the oldest building in Crested Butte today. The town had a 2-million-gallon reservoir above town, a telephone line connecting with Gunnison, and a town square laid out like a plaza with lakes, shade trees and shrubbery. The Old Rock Schoolhouse was built in 1883, as was the Old Town Hall, both of which stand today.

Crested Butte prospered from silver mining, but it was the development of coke quality coal that gave it staying power. Howard Smith initiated development when he sold 320 acres of his coal land in 1881 to Colorado Coal and Iron, which later became Colorado Fuel and Iron (CF&I) of Pueblo. Smith had a way of investing big, well-financed coal interests in Crested Butte, and yet this great entrepreneur left Crested Butte in the mid-1880s to go east for business, never to return. Smith's mark on Crested Butte was indelible, however, as he had established coal as the lasting lifeblood of the town.

Crested Butte's first coal miners came from Scotland, Ireland, Cornwall, Germany and Wales. They were followed by Greeks, Italians, and Southern Europeans from Slavic countries. Dozens of coke ovens spewed smoke, the streams were polluted, and a film of coal dust covered the town. Such was the price of prosperity.

Ernest Ingersoll, a traveler, described Crested Butte in 1884: "...at night when the blaze of the coke ovens sends a ruddy glare upon the overhanging woodlands and the snug town, one can appreciate the far-seeing expectations leading the people to say that they live in the Pittsburgh of the West."

Rio Grande engineer Lewis Lathrop offered his observations: "Both anthracite and soft coal poured in never-ending streams from the surrounding mountains... Long banks of coke ovens made the night sky lurid with leaping red flames, and the sickening-sweet odor of coal being baked into coke hung heavily over the snow-covered town."

As the town grew, so did the threat of fires. Three major blazes swept through portions of town, consuming whole blocks. In 1890, a fire destroyed 15 businesses. In 1893 all of Elk Avenue was burned while fire fighters were hampered by frozen water lines. In a desperate effort to snuff the flames, firemen set a dynamite charge in a furniture store. The charge was too big, however, and while it stopped the fire, it also blew a hole in the old Town Hall and shattered every window in town. In 1901 a third major fire damaged much of the downtown and burned the Colorado Supply Company Store.

Despite occasional infernos, Crested Butte survived. When silver crashed in 1893, the town stayed alive even as its many promising satellite communities failed, one by one. Coal and coke continued to be in demand, and the biggest producer was CC&I's Big Mine. Tapping a vein between 10 and 20 feet thick, the Big Mine provided a steady output of high grade coal after it opened in 1894. In 1902, the Big Mine produced 1,000 tons of coal per day and employed 400 miners. It was the third largest mine in Colorado and produced the highest quality coal in the state.

The Bulkley mine, named for Frank Bulkley, a well-healed mining engineer, was another prominent mine. Opened in

CRESTED BUTTE CHRONICLE/PILOT

Avalanches were often the most devastating among the many dangers inherent in early mining in the Elk Mountains. Throughout Colorado they still claim victims almost every year.

CRESTED BUTTE HISTORICAL MUSEUM

Saloons were the hallmark of almost every mining town, and Crested Butte had its share. Men hoist glasses while a little girl shares floor space with a pair of spittoons.

1908, the mine produced a high grade of bituminous coal two miles south of town on the flank of Mt. Whetstone. A few cabins were built to house some of the miners, but most of the miners had to walk from Crested Butte.

In the winter this required breaking trail through deep snow, so the miners took turns in the front of a procession. When the lead man got tired, he stepped aside and allowed the next man to break trail, falling in at the end of the line where the trail was easy to walk and he could rest.

In 1912 an avalanche ripped down from Whetstone, flew over the head house and roared down the tram line where 10 men were clearing the tracks. Six men were carried 500 feet down the mountain and buried. The slide ran another 500 feet into the valley, sweeping a loaded coal car from the tracks. All the miners but one - 31-year-old Frank Orazem - were dug out

of the snow and survived the ordeal. Orazem died of injuries that night.

Other coal mines near Crested Butte included the Robinson, Pueblo, Horace, Pershing and Peanut. The Peanut had a narrow vein of anthracite coal, 18 inches to two feet, requiring miners to lie on their sides or dig on their knees, using gunny sacks or old car tires for cushions. Each mine had its peculiarities in the layout of veins, and each required special skills and risks for miners, some of whom started in the mines at 12 to 14 years of age.

Miners not only cut seams, they built track, installed roof supports, and loaded coal cars. In a bituminous mine, in good conditions, a miner could load 30-40 tons of coal per day by hand. In an anthracite mine the figure dropped to 10 tons. If conditions were poor, a miner might work all day to load a single car. They were paid only for the coal they cut and loaded, not for the sum of their labor, which was Herculean.

The miners, mostly poor immigrants trying to get a start in the "new country," were heavily exploited, especially by

Coke ovens on the south side of Crested Butte converted coal into coke, which was then shipped by rail to the steel mill in Pueblo. The coking process spewed smoke and ash into the clear Colorado air.

Working the ovens was a hot and dirty job.

CC&I, the town's largest employer. Lax safety standards, long hours and the inherent dangers of coal mining caused many casualties, if not in outright deaths through accidents, then through long-term, health-related illnesses.

When mine accidents occurred, the company was usually exonerated while the miner was blamed for carelessness. In the aftermath of a mine accident, the company often inquired after the condition of the mules rather than the miners. The mules cost $200, while the miner could always be replaced by another in the pool of willing workers.

CC&I was vilified for cutting wages during recessions in order to maintain dividends for stockholders. Mine bosses controlled the politics of the town, electing those who they knew would support their agendas. Labor organizers were black-listed, while scabs were given better jobs.

Strikes occurred, like the one in 1891 over a cut in pay. The miners stopped the exhaust fan at the Big Mine, allowing the chamber to fill with explosive gases. The mine owners called in "Doc" Shores, the famous Gunnison lawman, who tried to enter the town quietly by rail with 24 deputies, only to be met by gunfire from angry miners. In the ensuing battle for control of the town 36 strikers were wounded.

A strike in 1913-14, this one instigated by the United Mine Workers, continued for 18 months and caused the mines to close until 1915 while burdening Crested Butte with economic turmoil. It finally ended, but with few concessions to miners. A major strike in 1927 led by the International Workers of the World came on the heels of a 20 percent pay cut.

IWW organizer John Perko led 400 Crested Butte miners out of the Big Mine, the Bulkley and the Horace. CF&I reacted with an ultimatum that if the men didn't return, the Big Mine would be shut down. The miners capitulated in 1928. CF&I finally closed the big mine in 1952, having found a less expensive source of coal closer to its steel mills in Pueblo.

Crested Butte owes its existence to the coal miners. They came from many ethnic backgrounds, and although squabbles arose over issues of nationalism, eventually they all blended together as miners, a fellowship that transcended ethnic differences. Together facing the rigors of winter weather and cut off from the world, the miners of Crested Butte celebrated life

THE JOKERVILLE DISASTER

Built on coal lands sold to Colorado Coal and Iron (later Colorado Fuel & Iron) by Howard Smith, the Jokerville Mine became Crested Butte's largest bituminous coal producer in the early 1880s. By 1884, 120 miners were digging coke quality coal from inside the Jokerville to feed 154 coke ovens. Conditions were dangerous at the Jokerville, as attested to in 1883, when a gas explosion killed one miner and burned six others, but CC&I dismissed it.

At 7 a.m. on the morning of January 24, 1884, the night shift of miners was being replaced by the day shift. At 7:30, once the shift was at work and relieved miners were resting at home over breakfast, a great explosion shattered the stillness of the town. Smoke billowed from the shaft of the Jokerville Mine and the families and friends of miners raced to the site with dread in their hearts.

The explosion had destroyed 100 feet of the tipple leading into the mine and ruined one of the exhaust fans ventilating the mine. Several outbuildings were burning. Fire roared from the mine entrance. Many prayers were said by those in waiting as one of the worst mining disasters in the history of the West began to unfold.

There was only one bright moment, when a band of miners rushed out of the mine to be greeted by a roar of cheers. Miner John Cashion, who was 1,800 feet from the entrance when the blast occurred, led ten others to safety. They groped along the passage, stumbling over obstacles, including the corpses of their peers, until they reached the entrance and burst out into the fresh air. Another group of miners, after surviving the initial blast, made it to within 200 feet of the

Conditions in coal mines were brutal for miners who worked long hours chipping coal from a seam, hand-loading ore carts, and coping with the threats of cave-ins, toxic gases and long-term health problems.

COLORADO HISTORICAL SOCIETY

mine entrance. But because the ventilation fan was destroyed, they ran out of air and, with the entrance in sight, they all succumbed to suffocation.

Miners came from around the region to help with the rescue, but to no avail, and 36 hours after the blast, 34 badly mangled bodies were taken from the mine. Another ten bodies were retrieved by February 2.

A funeral procession made up of a majority of Crested Butte citizens and a large delegation from Gunnison tramped quietly through three feet of snow to the cemetery, following sleighs bearing coffins. The victims were buried in a mass grave with the following inscription: "Their lives were gentle, and the elements so mixed in them that nature might stand up and say to all the world 'They were men.'" A coroner's jury assessed the cause of the disaster as a gas explosion and placed the blame on an unknown individual who had entered a closed chamber against the rules of the company and the instructions of the fire boss. This favorable outcome for the company was rendered by a jury foreman who was an employee of CC&I. He had selected three close friends of the mine superintendent for the jury.

Critics called the findings a whitewash and charged that CC&I was culpable for the disaster because of lax inspections and poor safety measures. It was widely known that the mine foreman had visited the mine only six times in the past year because he viewed the Jokerville as unsafe. The mine was never reopened and came to symbolize all that was hazardous about the coal business and corrupt about the town's largest mine employer.

The Big Mine, Crested Butte's largest, longest-running coal mine, occupied the "Bench" area below Gibson Ridge on the south side of town along with the row of coke ovens. All was owned by the Colorado Fuel & Iron Company.

Prospectors came to the "north country" of the Elk Mountains in the early 1860s. Braving hostile Utes, they sheltered in crude log cabins while searching for precious metals.

The Smith Hill Mine

Crested Butte's founding father, Howard Smith, opened Smith Hill Mine four miles up the Slate River from Crested Butte in 1881. The mine was perched on a hill 1,600 feet above the glacial valley, and with it a small town named Cloud City. The name was changed to Anthracite when the town was incorporated by late summer of 1881, and the following year the Rio Grande completed a spur to Smith Hill, where a 1,628-foot tram, the longest and steepest in Colorado, delivered coal to a huge coal crusher.

Smith leased the Smith Hill Mine to the Whitebreast Coal Company of Iowa, a company in which John C. Osgood later had a major interest, which then leased it to CF&I's predecessor. Anthracite soon had a population of 200, a school, post office, and library. In addition to harsh living conditions on the windswept hill, an avalanche swept through the town in 1883, killing six miners and injuring 15.

with polka dances. Accordion music enlivened the town through the late 1960s, and still does on special occasions today.

With the closing of the mines and the tearing up of the Rio Grande tracks in 1955, Crested Butte struggled through uncertain years with only a marginal economy. The streets were dirt and the population dwindled as residents sought work elsewhere. The American Smelting and Refining Company reopened the old Keystone Mine on the side of Mt. Emmons west of town in the early 1950s and built a large plant. The heavy metals mine revitalized the town for a while, but never enough to offset the loss of coal.

In 1958, Dr. Hubert Smith, a lawyer and MD from Texas, established the Law Science Academy to host summer recreational activities and cultural and scientific exchanges. The biggest change came in the early 1960s when a ski area was developed on Crested Butte Mountain and grew into the resort town of Mt. Crested Butte. The East River Valley shrugged off its mining heritage and embraced a new economy based on scenery, skier days and land development.

The traditional mining economy of Crested Butte seems dead and gone, but there is still considerable coal in the Crested Butte area. And, in 1977 AMAX, a major international mining company, announced the discovery of a 300-million-ton orebody of molybdenum, a steel strengthening alloy.

Nonetheless, coal production was strong and steady, averaging 5,000 tons of coal per month, until 1903, when the mine was temporarily closed and Anthracite miners moved to Crested Butte where they were employed at the Big Mine.

The Anthracite operated only intermittently after 1903, but had one last revival in the 1940s when its 400,000-ton waste dump was bought by the Empire Zinc and American Smelting and Refining Companies. The dump materials were used for a steel fluxing process and provided employment for several years.

The Smith Hill railroad spur was torn up in 1947 and all operations on Smith Hill ceased. Cattle graze on Smith Hill today, and a scattering of old buildings attests to 66 years of activity at Cloud City.

Gothic

The biggest boom town in the "north country" was Gothic (9,500 feet), nine miles north of Crested Butte. Called the "City of Silver Wires," Gothic grew to prominence at the confluence of Copper Creek and East River. Despite its great flourish, the town has always been humbled beneath 12,625-foot Gothic Peak, one of "The Crested Buttes" identified by Ferdinand Hayden.

Rich silver strikes were made in the Gothic area in the 1870s by John and David Jennings, who were grubstaked by Chicagoan Obediah Sands, a wealthy former hotel owner who had come west to improve his failing health. Sands was running out of money, but he took a gamble with the Jennings brothers, who were

The Sylvanite Mine was the biggest producer of silver for Gothic, "town of the silver wires." Stalagmites of ice are sprouting from the floor of the Sylvanite shaft.

about to enter the Gunnison country. He would take half of what they found.

What they found was one of the richest silver mines in the Gunnison country, the Sylvanite Mine. Their discovery brought hoards of miners to Gothic in the wild mining rush of 1879-80. The town was incorporated in July 1879. Two saw mills struggled to keep up with the demand for lumber. By winter of that year, 200 buildings had been erected and Gothic had a look and promise of permanence. There was a population of nearly 1,000 in Gothic or its immediate surroundings, and two silver smelters were nearing completion.

Only 26 families endured the frigid temperatures and snow six feet deep that winter of 1879-80. Their only connection with the outside world came by mail, carried by Louis Barthell, one of a hardy breed of skiing mailmen. The spring of 1880 regenerated the boom of the previous summer as thousands of transient miners sought a strike in the nearby mountains. By that summer, Gothic had five law firms, four grocery stores, three restaurants, two general stores, a bank, three doctors, two hotels and many saloons.

A Gothic newspaper vying for prominence ridiculed Gunnison as "dead and dull as a corpse. It has no ores, no mine, no resources of any kind. It is cold in winter and hot as blazes in summer. It is the dustiest hole in the universe." The Gunnison *Daily Review-Press* fired back that Gunnison had a population of 5,000 while "Gothic has not five hundred, counting all the yellow dogs."

This reference may have been to impugn Chinese laborers; there was persecution, and one Chinese laundryman was hanged in Gothic in the early 1880s for daring to compete with the white washer women of the town.

Former President U.S. Grant visited Gothic in 1880 to see a real mining camp in full swing. He was met by a marching band, a huge explosion of black powder, and a reception, plus visits to several mines. During its second summer, Gothic served as a major supply point for surrounding mines, with 400-500 "jacks" leaving town regularly for pack trips into the scattered mountain camps or over Pearl Pass to Aspen.

The Crested Butte and Gothic Toll Road was built in 1880 from Crested Butte to Gothic. The Aspen, Maroon Creek, Gothic Toll Road was built in the early 1880s as a means of connecting Gothic with Aspen. Stages delivering mail and passengers ran up Copper Creek, over East Maroon pass, and down Maroon Creek to Aspen. During winter, leather upholstered, four-seater sleds crossed the 11,800-foot pass.

Like most boom towns, Gothic's fortunes faded. The high cost of shipping ore, the failure to build a smelter, and the dropping cost of silver, all conspired to make the town uneconomical. By 1883 Gothic was failing, and by 1893, the year of the Silver Crash, the town was mostly deserted.

Unlike most mining towns facing desertion, Gothic was never a ghost town. Gothic was acquired in 1928 by the Rocky Mountain Biological Laboratory (RMBL) through the initiative of Dr. John C. Johnson, a professor of biology at Western State College who envisioned an outdoor classroom for biology students engaged in field studies in the pristine reaches of the Elk Mountain Range.

Today Gothic remains a center for learning in the old but renovated buildings. The program attracts well-known educators and researchers, foremost of whom is Dr. Paul Ehrlich, a scientist and outspoken author. RMBL holds summer sessions, and the old town swarms with young students performing long-term research on mountain ecosystems, entomology, acid rain and other studies.

GUNNISON PIONEER MUSEUM

Garwood H. Judd.

The Man Who Stayed

Garwood Hall Judd is remembered as "the man who stayed." Long after Gothic was abandoned to the ravages of nature, he remained as the town's only human resident.

Judd was born in 1852 in Ohio. He was 27 when he arrived in 1880 at the beginning of Gothic's boom days, and he quickly changed careers from miner to saloonkeeper. He was in Gothic when ex-President U.S. Grant visited. He would later become the permanent mayor of Gothic and was referred to by historian Lois Borland, a professor at Western State College, as "one of her friends in high places."

Judd was reputed to be well-educated, judging by his manner of speech and his having attended Oberlin College. He kept a typewriter in the back room of his cabin to write letters, still hoping to attract capital to reopen the mines at Gothic. After the town was deserted, Judd remained as a caretaker for properties and a kind of real estate agent.

By the 1920s, he had lived in Gothic for almost 50 years and entertained visitors with stories about the old mining days. Running a gauntlet of avalanche chutes beneath Gothic Peak, Judd would ski to Crested Butte to bring in supplies. He lived by modest means in the town where he alone was magistrate and citizen.

Judd was featured in a 1928 Fox Film Company feature and received a small stipend for his role as the mayor of Gothic, by then a ghost town. Garwood H. Judd remained in Gothic until his death in 1930 at 78 years old. His ashes were scattered around the townsite. The rushing falls above town on Copper Creek bear his name, as does a bench for those who choose the place for tranquil meditation.

Schofield

Mining activity in the Elk Mountains spawned many mining camps and fledgling towns. Strikes in the upper reaches of Rock Creek, or the Crystal River as it's known today, created the town of Schofield. Located in a narrow valley between Schofield Pass and the Devil's Punchbowl, Schofield was one of the earliest camps in the "north country" of the Elks. The town was platted in August 1879 by a group of men lead by B. F. Schofield.

The snow bridge across the Crystal River below the Devil's Punchbowl. This was a treacherous road when it was built in 1879 and remains treacherous today.

The townsite had been a camp six years before, and was seen by Henry Gannett, one of Ferdinand Hayden's "Rover Boys," when he explored the region in 1873. At that time, reported Gannett, there was only one other settlement in the Elks, and that was far to the southeast in Union Park.

Schofield was on the fringe of westward expansion. It was settled by daring men who braved hostile Ute Indians and harsh conditions in the high mountains. Their pluck was the stuff of legend, and by 1880 Schofield had 30 buildings, two sawmills and a large freighting operation to support the hundreds of miners searching the area for silver. In 1881 it was reported that Schofield had 50 frame buildings, two stores, four saloons, two restaurants, three real estate and mining brokers offices, one shoe shop, a livery stable and a population of 300, with upwards of 1,000 miners coming into the camp for supplies.

A jail was built in 1881 and it was tested by none other than the sheriff himself. The men of the town got the sheriff drunk, locked him in the jail, and despite his oaths, left him there until they were certain the jail would hold. By 1882 Schofield was granted a post office. Prominent mines near Schofield were the Shakespeare, Pride of the West, Oxford Belle and the North Pole.

The most exciting moment occurred in 1880 when ex-President U. S. Grant visit-

This two-store outhouse in Crested Butte proves that snows were deep in the "north country" .

ed Schofield on his tour of mining camps in the Elk Mountains. Grant had already visited Gunnison, Irwin, Crested Butte and Gothic, and he stopped by Schofield enroute to Crystal.

The miners of the town decided their prospects would be enhanced if Grant owned shares of one of their mines, so they attempted to "lose" him some shares in a poker game. That ruse failed, so one of the miners renowned for his corn whiskey attempted to get Grant drunk enough to become an investor. That ruse failed also, with the hard-drinking Grant leaving town no shares the richer.

Grant then navigated the treacherous Devil's Punchbowl, a cliff-hanger of a road through deep and narrow Crystal Canyon above the boiling whitewater of the Crystal River. Several miners who accompanied Grant told him the road through the canyon was called "Son-of-a-Bitch Canyon." Grant thought up a more appropriate name and suggested it be called Schurz Canyon for his political foe, Carl Schurz.

Schofield was abandoned, the victim of isolation and low-grade ore. The post office was closed in 1885, and despite a brief mining revival in 1899 by a group of Aspen investors, Schofield became a ghost town whose population migrated several miles down Crystal Canyon to Crystal City. Today Schofield has real estate potential as a mountain enclave where lots are being sold from the old town plat. Several small log houses have been built as summer-only accommodations.

Elko

As early as 1869, Willis McGlothlen had boldly entered Ute lands in the "north country" of the Elk Mountains and prospected. He and thirty men established a camp in 1872 near a picturesque lake in a mountain basin just west of Schofield Pass. The camp later became Elko. The first cabin in Elko was built the following year, and in 1875 the famous surveyor George Wheeler passed through and noted "the embryo village of Elko."

By 1881 Elko's population had grown to 300. The town was platted and had a sawmill, a $100,000 ore concentrator, a grocery store, assay office, shoe store and post office. Mines in the area were named the Monitor, Mountain Boy, Cameron, Osceola, Lake View, Cinnamon Pride and Hard Cash. By 1884 Elko had fallen victim to isolation and low-grade ores and was deserted. The town vanished over the ensuing decades.

Pittsburgh

Seven miles north of Crested Butte on the Slate River, the town of Pittsburgh grew up around rich silver, gold, copper and galena mines. Pittsburgh, named for its location among large coal deposits, became the population center for two failed camps, Oh-Be-Joyful, later named Tuscon, and Hidalgo, also known as Silver Cliff.

Pittsburgh was established in 1881 with a scattering of cabins, a post office, store and combination assayer-survey office. A population of 50 men worked in nearby mines, the Excelsior, the Black Queen and the famous Augusta, all of which were located in Oh-Be-Joyful valley to the west.

Access to the mines up the steep valley was prohibitive to all but burros, which hauled the ore out in long strings. Winter access was even more daunting because of the threat of avalanche. In January 1886 a huge slide swept away the bunk house and a cabin at the Excelsior mine. The bunkhouse was unoccupied, but four men were in the cabin. One escaped after exhaustive digging. With the muted voices of his comrades in his ears, he went to Pittsburgh for help. Rescuers came too late, however, for the men had suffocated beneath the snow.

In February 1904, nine miners who had had enough of winter, decided to leave the Augusta mine and snowshoe to

Crested Butte through two feet of fresh snow. One mile below the mine they were caught in a major slide churning with boulders and logs. Three of the men were carried on the cresting wave of the avalanche to the foot of the mountain. Aside from bruises, they were unharmed. The other six men perished beneath 20 feet of snow.

Pittsburgh grew steadily, and by 1886 had daily stage service to Crested Butte, a saw mill, two stores, two boarding houses, 25 cabins, a post office, saloons and a peak population of 200. Though the surroundings mines were rich and produced $1 million in silver, the climate and topography killed Pittsburgh. Avalanches destroyed many of the mine properties in the Oh-Be-Joyful valley.

Elkton

Built on the site of Minersville, one of the earliest mining camps in the Elk Mountains and the site of a massacre of 12 miners by Ute Indians in 1862, the town of Elkton in Washington Gulch was renowned for its neat orderliness and a prohibition against saloons and gambling houses. Minersville had been one of the first strikes in the Gunnison country in 1861, and a million dollars worth of gold had been panned and sluiced from nearby streams

The town of Elkton, named after the Elk Mountains, was established in 1880, and by the following year had a post office and half a dozen mines, the most profitable of which was the Painter Boy, which produced $100,000 worth of silver.

By 1885 it became obvious to investors

Gold panning was the first step in establishing a strike. If traces of gold were picked up, full-scale placer mining ensued. Such were the beginnings of mining in the Gunnison Country.

that the silver ore being mined there was low-grade, and they withdrew their investments. The town shut down shortly thereafter, and a fire in 1893 burned most of the buildings.

The Early Days of Skiing

Since the Elk Mountains were inundated by deep snow for at least seven months of the year, skis were widely used as the most sensible form of personal transportation. The "snowshoers," as they were called, employed long, unwieldy boards strapped to their feet with leather bindings. They carried a single, stout pole, which was used like a rudder. Turning was limited to stemming or the telemark turn, but most skiers went straight down, holding the pole alongside them for stability.

The *Elk Mountain Pilot* of Irwin reported that "every man, woman and child had to learn to ski or snowshoe ... if we wanted to go anywhere. All outlying districts were inhabited in those days... If residents wanted to come to the big town,

Skiers, or "Snowshoers," were many in the 1880s, as the long boards were the most efficient means of personal transportation during long winter months. These snowshoers are from Irwin in March 1883.

Crested Butte, they had to come on skis...it was not an uncommon sight to see fifty or more pairs of skis in front of M. J. Gray's store while miners and their wives were inside buying goods."

Ministers brought religion to the mining camps on skis, and skiing mailmen brought news from the outside world, each facing the dangers of extreme cold and deadly avalanches. Al Johnson was the most famous skiing mailman of the Crested Butte area. He made a regular run over Schofield Pass to Crystal City through the infamous Devil's Punchbowl.

Johnson, referred to as "the top snowshoer of the Rocky Mountains", approached his job as if it were a high-risk sport. The Devil's Punchbowl is a steep canyon where many avalanches funnel to the bottom. During times of avalanche danger, Johnson would point his skis straight down the deadly ravine and "let 'em rip." Miraculously, he survived many such perilous crossings to Crystal.

Another amazing set of skiers were the professional packers, men who carried 100-pound loads to mining camps in winter. These hardy skiers navigated treacherous mountain passes on long boards weighted down with supplies for which they charged by the pound.

The best backcountry skiing conditions occurred in the spring, at night or early in the morning, when the snow was consoli-dated and a crust had formed. For uphill travel, the skier either removed his boards and pulled them up the hill with rope, or sprinkled water on the base and created a gripping surface of ice and snow. Smoked glasses were worn to prevent snow blindness from the intense reflection of the sun, and some skiers smeared their faces with a water and gunpowder paste to keep their skin from blistering.

By the early 1880s, skiing had become more than utilitarian. It was a sport. Races were held where contestants challenged a course straight down a mountain. Racing skis were prepared with bee's wax rubbed into the bottom and polished for a fast running surface. Spectators from different camps lined the course to cheer on their favorites as they plummeted down a steep, challenging course.

One of the earliest races was held in Irwin in January 1881 and featured 25 contestants who raced down a quarter-mile course into town for $25 in prize money. Most of the skiers failed to cross the finish line, either flopping into deep snow just after the start or losing their skis in mid-air on a jump and landing head-first in the snow.

Skiing became popular in many of the mining camps, wherever there was plenty of snow and a jovial sense of fun. By the mid-1880s, the Gunnison country was renowned as a center for skiing, with Crested Butte as its primary focus. Spectators came by train to see the exhibitions.

The biggest ski race of the early days occurred in Crested Butte on February 22, 1886 in honor of Washington's birthday. Prize money was put up by Crested Butte, and racers convened from all the mining camps. A delegation selected the hill, just south of Crested Butte on Gibson Ridge, where racers would run a straight downhill 525 yards long. The slope was 35 degrees, and anybody who made it down the incline would then have to cross 250 feet of flats before reaching the finishing line.

A special train was chartered from Gunnison for spectators, and skiers trekked from miles around to cheer their favorites. After several heats, with four skiers abreast, the finalists were Charlie Baney of Crested Butte, Al Johnson and Al Fish of Crystal City, and Harry Cornwall of Irwin. The final heat was winner-take-all for a $20 purse and the title "Champion Skier of the Rocky Mountains."

At the rifle shot that announced the start, the skiers took off down the mountain. Baney, a 16-year-old, who had practically been raised on skis, and Al Johnson, the famous skiing mailman, gained the lead.

They were neck and neck, but Baney, in a tuck, was first to cross the finish line, by two feet, with both skiers going 60 miles per hour. Johnson and Baney hugged, received their awards, and the entire town celebrated the day with a polka party of historic proportions.

As the mining camps failed during the late 1880s, so did the ski races. A long hiatus would occur until skiing became not only a winter pastime but a major economic factor for the Elk Mountains.

In the 1950s, Western State College ski competitors trained at Rozman Hill under the guidance of ski coach Sven Wiik. The WSC Mountaineers ranked high in collegiate standings.

Only the brave...These early mountain bikers pose at the top of 12,700 foot Pearl Pass in the mid-1970's enroute to Aspen during one of the early Pearl Pass bicycle tours.

Mt. Crested Butte and the Skiing Boom

Skiing got off the ground as a commercial venture in the Elk Mountains in 1960, when Dick Eflin and Fred Rice, both from Kansas, bought the Malensek ranch north of Crested Butte and announced plans to build a major recreation center on Crested Butte Mountain (12,162 feet). This ambition would later transform a mountain ranch into the town of Mt. Crested Butte.

By the winter season of 1962-63, Crested Butte Ski Area boasted a gondola, the first in Colorado, ski trails, a base area that included old ranching buildings, and the humble beginnings of a promising recreation economy. In the winter of 1965-66 the ski area fell under financial duress and went through a series of bankruptcies. The turnaround came in 1970 when the fledgling resort was purchased by Howard "Bo" Callaway, a wealthy Georgian who later served as Secretary of the Army under Presidents Nixon and Ford.

Callaway had a great vision for Crested Butte, and he and investors poured $20 million into improvements,

Mules were the transportation system for moving freight through the mountains to mines and camps. A typical mule train had 150 animals carrying at least 50 pounds each. Lumber, being packed here, is bound for one of the remote mines.

expansions, new lifts, land development and environmental requirements. The town of Mt. Crested Butte was incorporated in 1973 to form a community around the new ski resort whose popularity soared during the 1970s.

Today, Crested Butte Mountain Resort is one of the ten biggest ski areas in Colorado. The ski area covers 1,160 total skiable acres, with some of the most demanding double-black diamond runs of any ski area in the U.S. CBMR served 519,250 skiers in 1996-97 with 14 lifts. There are 5,000 lodging units in Crested Butte and Mt. Crested Butte. The ski area is the main revenue producer for the Crested Butte region.

Birthplace of the Mountain Bike

Crested Butte is one of two communities in the U.S. credited with inventing the mountain bike. Marin County, California is the other. Crested Butte shared in giving birth to the mountain bike as a utilitarian and recreational vehicle that has gained worldwide popularity.

Since most of the town's streets were rough dirt roads as late as the 1980s, the town was well-suited to fat tires. Crested Butte is also characterized for a healthy, athletic, young population. Strong skiers and hikers, these modern

day mountain folk also embraced bicycles. By the early 1970s, they employed sturdy, fat-tired one speed "paperboy" bikes as all terrain vehicles, pedaling and pushing them over high passes and trails in the Elk Mountains.

In 1976, the first annual Pearl Pass Bicycle Tour came about as a challenge. A group of motorcycle riders from Aspen crossed rugged Pearl Pass to Crested Butte's infamous Grubstake Bar, where they celebrated their achievement with some enthusiasm. The Crested Butte contingent responded by riding back over Pearl Pass, employing only pedal power, kegs of beer, and some serious chest-beating.

The Pearl Pass Tour spawned a lasting tradition as growing numbers of mountain bikers rode to Aspen over the 12,700 foot pass every September during the height of fall colors.

One tour, including a camp just below timberline in Cumberland Basin, had over 300 participants.

A group of riders from Marin County used the annual tour as a proving ground for their innovations on the demanding terrain. The traditional one speeds were fitted with caliper brakes, knobby tires, and gearing. By the late 1970s, mountain bike races were held in association with the tour, and media capitalized on the event. The sport was promoted, and in the 1980s mountain biking exploded as the fastest growing part of the American cycling industry.

As innovations made mountain bikes more versatile, the terrain available to Crested Butte mountain bikers expanded dramatically. Bikers began riding every game, hiking and 4-wheel-drive trail in the Elk Mountains. This prompted the Forest Service to close off designated Wilderness areas to all "mechanized" vehicles.

Today, Crested Butte remains one of the premier mountain biking locations in the world, attracting thousands of cyclists to its challenging trails and unparalleled mountain vistas. Coming full circle, a cult of Crested Butte riders has brought back the one-speed, fixed-gear, 28-inch wheeled bikes from a century ago.

The Mountain Bike Hall of Fame, located in the Crested Butte Mountain Heritage Museum, tells the story with photographs, articles and displays of early mountain bikes.

Crested Butte Mountain Heritage Museum

Historic photographs and artifacts from Crested Butte's early days to the present are represented in the Heritage Museum in a restored miner's home at 200 Sopris in downtown Crested Butte. The museum offers a glimpse of the past, from the Ute Indians to the current day recreation-based economy. An early day kitchen has been preserved in one of the museum rooms. A walking tour of town is available.

The Mountain Bike Hall of Fame features memorabilia and bicycles from the early days of mountain biking. The Hall of Fame honors mountain biking personalities who have been important leaders in the sport.

For information, call (970) 349-1880.

Crested Butte to Kebler Pass

The 30-mile-long Kebler Pass road follows Coal Creek west from Crested Butte and climbs gradually past the old Keystone Mine. It is the only unpaved section remaining on the entire 204 miles of the West Elk Loop. Winter plowing ends here and only skiers and snowmobiles travel beyond through the deep snows of winter. The summer-only dirt road follows the old Rio Grande railroad grade toward Kebler Pass and the mining camps of Irwin and Ruby, the lumber camp of Telco and the coal mining town of Floresta. Near the pass the road forks left to Ohio Pass and Gunnison, or goes straight over Kebler Pass and into the Anthracite Creek drainage, meeting Highway 133 at Crystal Meadows, just below the Paonia Reservoir Dam.

The Mt. Emmons Project

Two miles west of Crested Butte, on the flank of Mt. Emmons (12, 392 feet), is the Mt. Emmons Project at the site of the historic Keystone Mine. A former silver mine that closed after the Silver Crash of 1893, the mine was revived in the 1950s by the American Smelting and Refining Company, which later sold its interest to a major international mining conglomerate, American Metals at Climax, or AMAX.

In 1977 AMAX announced plans to mine 300 million tons of molybdenum ore from the third largest known "moly" orebody in the world, which lies beneath Mt. Emmons and Red Lady Bowl.

Julian A. Kebler, for whom Kebler Pass is named, was a mining engineer for the Colorado Fuel & Iron Company.

KEBLER PASS

Kebler Pass is named for Julian Kebler, one of Osgood's chief lieutenants and president of the Colorado Fuel and Iron Company of Pueblo, which had acquired the coal lands of the Ruby-Anthracite region in the early 1887. His acquisition was instrumental in convincing the Rio Grande to extend tracks from Crested Butte to Floresta. Kebler, a brilliant MIT engineer, with financial magnate John C. Osgood pioneered the successful industrial development of Colorado.

Kebler Pass is 9,980 feet. The road, mostly gravel, is closed in the winter. In spring and summer the pass offers a splendid display of Colorado wildflowers, from daisy to columbine.

An artist's rendering from anti-mine advocates in Crested Butte during the late 1970s illustrated the possible subsidence from the AMAX mining Project once the 300-million-ton molybdenum orebody was removed from Mt. Emmons.

The late John Denver made several appearances in Crested Butte during the campaign against AMAX. Denver and other celebrity environmentalists supported the town's position against the mine.

Molybdenum is a steel-strengthening alloy used in high-tech metals with strategic military value for its use in jet fighters and rocket nose cones. Moly is also used in lightweight, high-performance applications like bicycle frames.

In the 70's AMAX planned for massive tailings or waste dumps to fill an alpine valley. Low-grade ore was to be produced at the rate of 20,000 tons per day. The mine was projected to double the population of Gunnison County with a huge construction force and a full-time mining crew. The socio-economic impacts of the mine were to be considerable.

This large scale industrial development was hotly contested by the new breed of Crested Butte resident who arrived from the 1960s through the '80s. A pitched debate ensued in the town where many old-time miners argued that AMAX would return Crested Butte to the "good old days" of a steady paycheck for an honest day's work.

On a tour of "boom towns" in the west sponsored by AMAX in 1979, Gunnison County officials learned that crime rates soar, services (schools, police, medical, etc.) are overburdened and the traditional values of a community are diluted by a sudden influx of population. A dim mood of despair permeates boom towns unable to cope with rapid change brought on by a huge wave of itinerant laborers.

It was more than a "not in my back yard" argument. Colorado had learned that such growth carried a high price tag; impact mitigation had become a matter of state policy and would have been applied to the Mt. Emmons Project, raising the cost to AMAX.

There were negative environmental aspects; toxic, wind-blown tailings, insatiable consumption of water, fossil fuel pollution and water table contamination, all of which can occur from the process of gutting a mountain and extracting a huge volume of low-grade ore. Since the mining days of old, Crested Butte had become a well-established resort where ambiance was all-important. Residents feared that a major industrial development would clash with the established economy while creating a repugnant exploitation of the land.

Despite the rights granted to mining companies under the powerful 1872

Mining Law, the town challenged AMAX on every front, including a heated campaign waged in the local and national media. The town championed the ideals of environmental protection and small town autonomy, becoming the David to the AMAX Goliath. Crested Butte fought AMAX in the courts, challenging water allocations and the myriad social impacts the mine might create.

A major Environmental Impact Statement was prepared by the Forest Service evaluating the many changes AMAX would bring to the county. In 1983, after six years of intense controversy, AMAX announced the Mt. Emmons Project would be postponed.

The adversity of Crested Butte was one reason, but the main issue was a decline in the metals market. Molybdenum slumped, the orebody lost value, and the company decided to wait for a stronger market and a less enthusiastic adversary.

In typical fashion, Crested Butte held a street dance to celebrate the decision. A group of citizens who had rallied against the mine hiked and biked to the top of Mt. Emmons, where a cheer went up across the Elk Mountains that AMAX was beaten, at least for the time being. Fifteen years later, in January 1998, AMAX, now merged as Cyprus-Amax, announced a new mining plan to Crested Butte and Gunnison County.

Following a seven-year permit process, the company plans to mine 10,000 tons of molybdenum ore per day for up to 25 years. This "small mine" option targets 200 million tons of the highest grade ore. Cyprus-Amax plans

Irwin in the early days shows a promising town in the midst of the "north country" of the Elk Mountains. The Presbyterian Church was the largest church in the Gunnison country when it was built in 1882.

to store tailings in Splains Gulch, a valley near the mine site, where the sludge would be piped until the mining operations are complete, at which time up to 60 percent of the tailings would be piped back into the mine cavern and used as back-fill. A large amount of tailings would remain in Splains Gulch, stored in a "lined surface impoundment." Cyprus-Amax proposes a production work force of 350 for its current plans.

Telco, Splains Gulch

Just below the top of Kebler Pass, in an open glade, was the site of The Endner Lumber Company, TELCO, which opened in 1917 and at one time employed 30 men and produced a million board feet of lumber annually. Timber for the mill was skidded from Splains Gulch. A railroad siding, boarding house, barns, cabins and a blacksmith shop stood until 1929, when the Rio Grande discontinued its Floresta spur.

Irwin and Ruby Gulch

Three miles northwest of Telco, on the road to Lake Irwin, lie the remains of the once thriving mining camp of Irwin. The town was transformed from a frontier camp into a booming mining town by Richard Irwin, a prospector who had been up and down the Rockies, and even to

Miners at the Forest Queen Mine in 1883, one of the most important silver mines of Irwin.

The rough streets of Irwin are indicative of the frontier aspect of the town as it boomed in the early 1880s.

Nome, Alaska, searching for strikes. As a young man Irwin had ridden for the Pony Express. Before venturing into the Gunnison Country he had served a term in the State Legislature from Custer County on the eastern plains of Colorado.

Irwin packed silver ore from Ruby Gulch, where the townsite would later be located, on burros to Alamosa in 1879. The ore was assayed at $3,000 a ton. Both his reputation and that of the region were made. That winter, when a total of 40 feet of snow fell on miners (Kebler Pass routinely receives some of the highest snowfall of any place in Colorado), they ran low on supplies and had to ski over 10,032-foot Ohio Pass to restock. These staunch men trekked back over the pass with 18-foot skis and 100-pound packs in order to maintain their claims.

Before the snow could melt out in the spring of 1880, more provisions were being packed over Ohio Pass. A makeshift camp served as a supply depot at the bottom of the pass where a hotel was established in a tent. Its modest amenities included one long bed made of buffalo blankets and hay. Everybody slept in the same bed, sometimes even both sexes, but that caused little concern because only boots were removed for sleeping.

In 1880, ex-President U.S. Grant visited Irwin on an excursion to see for himself the promise and excitement of a real Rocky Mountain mining camp. Grant came into the Gunnison country from Saguache, traveled over Cochetopa Pass, was received in Gunnison, then headed north into the Elk Mountains to Irwin.

Because of the many southerners who

mined at the camp and hated Grant for what he had done to the South during the Civil War, a plot was hatched to kidnap the former President. When a kidnapping proved too difficult, the plotters decided to kill Grant. Irwin lay in a gulch, and the assassins planned to delay their victim on his way through town and induce him into making a speech. At that opportunity a women would approach and fire the fatal shot.

An actress in Irwin learned of the plot and informed her boyfriend miner. The miner feared retaliation if he blew the whistle on the conspirators, so he waited until the day of Grant's arrival. In desperation, he turned to Irwin's mayor, Ed Travers. Travers had been a Confederate soldier, hated Grant, and would have been "pleased to see the vile wretch who had brought so many tears, so much grief and woe to the land, assassinated, his very heart torn out." But Travers also didn't like the assassins. He was a man of integrity and determined that Grant should be protected while in his town.

Grant was met at the edge of Irwin and

escorted into town, without incident, by a wagon pulled by a pair of mules. On the wagon, in lieu of a brass band, was a kettle and bass drum. The publisher of the *Elk Mountain Pilot* reported on the entourage: "As the route was up a steep grade, the little old mules wheezed a bit in pulling the wagon and the drummers went a boom-de-boom, and rat-a-tatting on their drums. As I looked at General Grant, I could not help visioning his thoughts at that time. Just imagine, he had visited all of the crowned heads of the world, listened to classical music, and now, to think here he was riding behind two noisy drums going up a gulch of the Rocky Mountains of Colorado."

Grant visited Irwin for two days, but no assassination plot was carried out. He visited the mines and a stamp mill, and he was feted at a banquet. Later, he retired to the Irwin Club for drinks and relaxation. The Club was reputed to be a hall of perdition, with liquor and gambling, a place the married men in town frequented despite the rebukes of their wives.

Despite its scandalous, frontier element, Irwin embraced the trappings of civilized society. The first church in Irwin was the Presbyterian Church. When it was built in 1882 it was the largest church in Gunnison County, seating 350 worshippers and winning the notoriety of being the "highest church in Colorado." A school was also built in town, open during the summers to avoid the impossible winter conditions at over 10,000 feet.

The town was fitted with a municipal water system piped through a 500-foot tunnel from Lake Brennand and connect-

THE WORLD'S RECORD ELK RACK

Joe Plute was hunting in Dark Canyon on Anthracite Creek in 1899 when he bagged a huge elk. Its antlers spread more than 51 inches at the widest point, and the basal circumference of one antler was more than 12 inches. Two points of the record rack extended more than 25 inches.

According to the official Boon and Crockett Club, Plute had brought in the world's record elk rack, with a point rating of 442 and 3/8 points. But Plute didn't know that. He was a man of the mountains and thought little about world records. He gave the rack to Ed Rozich to pay for his bar bill, and the saloon was later inherited by Ed Rozman, who suspected the rack was a record.

It was Charles Whadford of the Hotchkiss Elk's Lodge who finally entered the rack into the ratings in 1961 at the American Museum of Natural History in New York. The rack was mounted on the largest head available by the American Sportsman's Club, and it was exhibited far and wide. The magnificent trophy was on display for many years at the Crested Butte Hardware and Conoco, and is currently on display at the Crested Butte Visitor Center.

ed to hydrants throughout the town. The water dropped 300 feet from the lake, creating tremendous water pressure in town. A mischievous miner passing through town noticed a store clerk using a hose to scrub the inside of his store. He

The huge coal breaker at Floresta was the largest west of Pennsyvlania. Built in 1898, it was capable of handling 2,000 tons of coal per day. Floresta produced a total 800,000 tons of coal from 1893 to 1918.

hurried to the lake and opened the valve wide, sending a burst of pressure through the hose. The store clerk was helpless to contain the powerful surge, spraying everything on the shelves.

Violence was a way of life in Irwin, where claim jumping was a common occurrence. A young man from Philadelphia, Robert Breckenridge, joined with two other miners at Irwin, William and James Edgley, who had a claim on Anthracite Creek west of Irwin. A few days after their departure, the bodies of the two brothers were found, each having been shot through the head. Their possessions were gone and so was Breckenridge, who was apprehended by a ten-man posse two days later near Pitkin, east of Gunnison.

Breckenridge was almost lynched on the spot after being caught with the dead brothers' possessions, but "Doc" Shores, a Gunnison lawman, persuaded the posse to turn him over to justice. Breckenridge's wealthy mother arrived soon afterwards from Philadelphia and gave favors to the city marshal and county sheriff. When a grand jury met for the trial, key witnesses were either not called or couldn't be found. Breckenridge went free. He returned to Philadelphia, where he wrote a feature article for a publication stating his plight at nearly being lynched for a crime he didn't commit.

Avalanche was another constant threat to the tranquillity of Irwin. In January 1883 a massive slide broke loose from Mt. Owen and swept over four mines, the Durango, Ruby Chief, Old Sheik and Howard Extension. Eight men were buried and the shaft houses were swept away. In February 1891 a slide 150 feet wide came off Ruby Peak and smashed the Bullion King mine. The miners had just left the boarding house and entered the shaft so they were spared. But the wife of the mine superintendent, a mother, her infant and a lodger were all buried and killed.

Despite the threat of Ute Indian attacks and deadly avalanches, by the summer of 1880 Irwin's population had swelled to 5,000.

One observer remarked, "I have never seen a community where money was so plentiful, everyone had a huge roll. Money came in so fast it looked as if making money was about the easiest thing in the world. We thought it would always continue."

It didn't. Even though Irwin expanded to swallow up neighboring camps its fame was fleeting. Despite its 23 saloons, 7 dance halls, houses of prostitution, and Windsor Hotel which attracted such patrons as U.S. Grant, John Jacob Astor, William Vanderbilt and Horace Tabor, by the late 1880s the boom was over. When silver was demonitized in 1893 the town died.

Irwin now has scattered cabins and a sparse population, only a handful of whom face the grueling winter and deep snows as year-round residents. These hearty folks commute to Crested Butte for work and supplies by snowmobile.

CAROL CRAVEN PHOTO

Two young deer are typical of the abundant wildlife travelers can see on Kebler Pass, or anywhere on the West Elk Loop.

Floresta

Between Kebler Pass (9,980 feet) and Ohio Pass (10,033 feet) the Rio Grande railroad line veered southwest and followed rolling contours to Floresta, a coal mine and town snugly tucked among the high peaks of Anthracite Ridge.

The coal fields of Floresta were acquired by J.A. Kebler in 1887, while working for J. C. Osgood. Later, after Osgood took over steelmaker Colorado Fuel & Iron, the company opened the Floresta mine. The Rio Grande spur from Crested Butte reached Floresta in 1893.

The fledgling town was issued a post office in 1897 and peaked with a population of 250. First called Ruby-Anthracite,

the name of the town was changed in 1901 to Floresta - Spanish for "forest" or "country estate."

In Floresta, anthracite ore was mined from 1893 to 1918. The largest coal breaker west of Pennsylvania was built in Floresta in 1898. It was 114 feet high and capable of handling 2,000 tons of coal per day.

Production never reached that level. Because of deep snow and dramatic winter weather that brought more than 20 feet of snow, Floresta operated only from July through January. It produced a total of 800,000 tons of coal and is today a ghostly ruin in a remote mountain basin.

Lake Irwin

Four miles before Kebler Pass is beautiful Lake Irwin, set beneath the mountain peaks of Ruby and Owen. A Forest Service Campground is on one end of the lake, and the Irwin Lodge stands above it. Built in 1974 and refurbished in 1979, the lodge is built of cedar and provides rooms and a restaurant and bar. During the summer, hikers and mountain bikers frequent

Quaking Aspen line both sides of the forest road across Kebler Pass, dramatic and beautiful every season, with Mt. Marcellina in the background.

the establishment. During winter, it is a haven for skiers and snowmobilers. A snowcat skiing service with powder guides offers skiing on 2,200 acres of National Forest.

Horse Ranch Park

Four miles west of Kebler Pass, beyond dense spruce forests, the valley opens at Horse Ranch Park. Here are the trail-heads for North Anthracite Creek, Oh-Be-Joyful Pass, the Dike Trail and Swampy-Beckwith Pass, some of the most dramatic country in the Elk Mountains.

The West Elk Wilderness flanks the Byway on the south; the Raggeds Wilderness is even closer on the north. High mountain peaks abound in every view.

In 1881, Horse Ranch park was a grazing area for the horses and teams of miners in the area. Two horse thieves once thought they'd have some easy pickings, so they gathered up as many horses as they could find and drove them down toward the present day Erikson Springs campground, where they were apprehended by an angry posse. In a gun battle, two of the thieves and one deputy were killed. The thieves were buried on the spot. The location of their unmarked graves is unknown.

The Big Quakies

The Kebler Pass aspen forest is one of the largest contiguous stands of aspen in the world, reputed to be the largest living organism on the planet. Aspen trees are clones that grow from a common root base. The "quakies" of Kebler Pass spread for many square miles of the forest. Many bear the signatures of shepherds, cowboys and hunters who carved them decades ago.

Erikson Springs

The expulsion of the Utes in 1881 opened the area to settlement; Billy Muncey and his friends arrived in the Anthracite Creek area near Mount Marcellina and went on into the Ragged Mountain region. He homesteaded, built a cabin, furnished it, and returned east to marry his sweetheart.

Approximately two years later he returned with his bride only to find that a cloudburst had unleashed a torrent of water that swept the house off its foundation. He stayed anyway and we have Muncey Creek, Muncey Basin and the Muncey stock driveway as a legacy.

Erik Erikson homesteaded the area at the confluence of Anthracite and Muncey Creeks in 1905. His family made many trips down the Anthracite Creek trail, crossing the creek 13 times to get to Somerset. From their place to Placita was 21 miles. In the winter they walked it on snowshoes.

Although it was earlier proposed as a railroad link, actual construction of the Kebler Pass road began in 1917 and took four years to complete. The Erikson Springs campground was traded to the government by Mr. Erikson in the 1940s. The cabin on the east side of the road is the original Erikson house, still used today.

Other early settlers included the Norris Family, the Howells, the Beezleys, the Gallobs, the Volks and the Bears. While the ranches began to change ownership in the mid-1950s many of the original homesteads are still standing.

Crystal Meadows

In the six-mile valley from Erikson Springs Campground to Crystal Meadows Ranch many families survived by growing potatoes and vegetable gardens, plus capitalizing on the excellent fishing and hunting. The wicked winters presented many challenges for the early pioneers.

By the early 1900's demand grew for a half-way place on the arduous trip from Paonia to the upper Muddy and Anthracite Creek area. In 1918 the Carl Berg family moved to the ranch at the corner of Muddy and Anthracite Creeks to begin a business of caring for weary travelers. Eighty years later Crystal Meadows Ranch still gives travelers a place to stay, eat or to take a break from driving.

The ranch was sold several times in the ensuing years. It has been owned by the current owners saince 1987. The name came from clear, sparkling Anthracite Creek and the beautiful meadow the ranch sits on.

It took 30 years for the government to approve the Paonia water project. Work was begun on the Paonia dam and reservoir in 1959. During the four years of construction the ranch was headquarters for the contractor. The large rock in the front yard rolled off the mountainside and bounced onto the grassy area sometime in the mid-1980's.

POINTS OF INTEREST
Crested Butte and Kebler Pass, 30 miles

• Crested Butte, many historic buildings. Visitor's Center is at the intersection of Highway 135 and Elk Ave; Historical Museum is in center of town at 200 Sopris.

• Highway continues 3 miles north to Mt. Crested Butte and the Crested Butte Ski Area.

• Crested Butte Mountain is east of town (12,172 feet).

• Gothic, at one time a bustling mining camp, is 8 miles north on the Gothic road. This is an access point to the high country including Schofield Pass, which is 4-wheel-drive only.

• West out of Crested Butte is County Road 12, the Kebler Pass road. It is 30 miles to the end of the West Elk Loop Scenic Byway. Mt. Emmons (12,392 feet) is on the north.

• Ruby, Irwin and other ghost towns are in the vicinity of Lake Irwin, mile 5.

• The Ruby-Irwin Cemetery and Mary Bambrough's grave are atop Kebler Pass, mile 7.

• Horse Ranch Park, mile 11, is the jumping off point for trails both north and south.

• Erikson Springs campground, Dark Canyon and Anthracite Creek, mile 24.

• Crystal Meadows is the end of the Byway, mile 30, at the base of Paonia Dam and reservoir. A kiosk with information panels about the West Elk Loop is located here.